PRAISE FOR *I AM MY [WIFE]*

"A remarkable piece of political theater . . . . . . play and the performance are an extraordinary stroke of theatrical transformation, unquestionably one of the most mesmerizing events of recent seasons . . . [The] writing is spare, elusive, and highly literate . . . Like Tony Kushner, [Doug Wright] has found a way to use his gay identity as a universal criticism of life."   —ROBERT BRUSTEIN, *The New Republic*

"The dramatic event of the year . . . Marvelous . . . Wright [has] deftly and poetically captured this outré, complex, and courageous person . . . An amazing theatrical experience."
     —DONALD LYONS, *New York Post*

"A theatrical essay, about the importance of recording history, that ends up challenging the reliability of all historical narratives, including its own."
     —DON SHEWY, *The New York Times*

"Astonishing . . . An altogether fascinating biography."
     —LINDA WINER, *Newsday*

"The writing is glorious throughout—sharp, funny, admiring, and full of ambivalence and wonder."
     —HEDY WEISS, *Chicago Sun-Times*

"Captivating . . . The ambiguities in Charlotte's story, while troubling to her admirers, only make her a more fascinating theatrical character. The sweet old lady who is really a sturdy old man is a symbol of the contradictions, concealment, and compromises that color even the most mundane lives."

—CHARLES ISHERWOOD, *Variety*

"Unique and deeply affecting."

—JACQUES LE SOURD, *The Journal News*

"A provocative slice of history told with considerable artistry."

—MICHAEL KUCHWARA, Associated Press

"Engrossing . . . *I Am My Own Wife* is a sharply crafted portrait that skips the obvious transvestite angle . . . to explore subtleties regarding quite a different sort of passion."

—MICHAEL SOMMERS, *The Newark Star-Ledger*

"Beguiling." —*Time Out New York*

JOAN MARCUS

DOUG WRIGHT

I AM MY OWN WIFE

Doug Wright won an Obie Award for outstanding achievement in playwrighting and the Kesselring Award for Best New American Play from the National Arts Club for his play *Quills*. He went on to write the screenplay adaptation, marking his motion picture debut. The film was named best picture by the National Board of Review and was nominated for three Academy Awards. His screenplay was nominated for a Golden Globe Award and received the Paul Selvin Award from the Writers Guild of America. Wright's stage work has been produced at New York Theatre Workshop, Lincoln Center, the WPA Theater, Geffen Playhouse, Wilma, Woolly Mammoth, the McCarter Theatre, and La Jolla Playhouse. His previous works include *The Stonewater Rapture*, *Interrogating the Nude*, *Watbanaland*, *Buzzsaw Berkeley*, and *Unwrap Your Candy*. Wright has been published three times in the *Best Short Plays* series, and his work has appeared in *The Paris Review*. He's a member of the Dramatists Guild; the Writers Guild of America, East; and the Society of Stage Directors and Choreographers. He serves on the board of the New York Theatre Workshop.

FABER AND FABER, INC.

An affiliate of Farrar, Straus and Giroux

New York

I AM
MY OWN
WIFE

Studies for a Play About the Life of

Charlotte von Mahlsdorf

. . .

DOUG WRIGHT

FABER AND FABER, INC.
An affiliate of Farrar, Straus and Giroux
19 Union Square West, New York 10003

Library of Congress Cataloging-in-Publication Data
Wright, Doug.
    I am my own wife : studies for a play about the life of Charlotte von
Mahlsdorf : a play / by Doug Wright.— 1st ed.
        p.   cm.
    ISBN 0-571-21174-7 (pbk. : alk. paper)
    1. Mahlsdorf, Charlotte von, 1928–2002—Drama.   2. Collectors and
collecting—Drama.   3. National socialism—Drama.   4. Transvestites—
Drama.   5. Communism—Drama.   6. Gay men—Drama.   7. Germany—
Drama.   I. Mahlsdorf, Charlotte von, 1928–2002.   II. Title.
    PS3573.R5325213 2004
    812'.54—dc22

                                                        2003021583

Designed by Gretchen Achilles

www.fsgbooks.com

3   5   7   9   10   8   6   4   2

FOR MY FOUR VERY DEDICATED "WIVES":

JEFFERSON MAYS, JOHN MARKS,

JEFFREY SCHNEIDER,

AND MOISÉS KAUFMAN

ACKNOWLEDGMENTS

For their tireless support in bringing Charlotte von Mahlsdorf all the way from East Berlin to the Broadway stage:

Robert Redford, Ken Brecher, Philip Himberg, Robert Blacker and the Sundance Theater Institute, Eric Rosen, Heather Schmucker and the About Face Theater Company in Chicago, Jim Nicola and the New York Theatre Workshop, Des McAnuff, Shirley Fishman, Carrie Ryan and the La Jolla Playhouse, Paul Lister and Dreamworks SKG, The Tectonic Theater Project, Blanka Zizka, Jiri Zizka and the Wilma Theater in Philadelphia, Tim Sanford, William Russo, Sonya Sobieski and Playwrights Horizons in New York, Carol Rigolot and the Council of the Humanities at Princeton University, the German Department of Vassar College, The MacDowell Colony, Yaddo, the staff of *Prinz Eisenherz Buchladen*, Drew Hodges and Spotco, Taylor-Wessig in Berlin, David Richenthal, Sarah Jane Leigh, Doug MacLaren, David Colden, Steve Simons, Marcus McGregor, Steven Roose, David Schmerler, Kent Eiler, Eva Longscharitsch, Joyce Ketay, Jason Baruch, Richard Kornberg, Sam Cohn, Denise Oswald, Debra Immergut, Christopher Ashley, Andreas Meier, Michael Borowski, Kenny Mellman, Justin Bond, David Hines, Lauren Landau, Mary Hines, Philip Sherwell, Matthew Shiner, James Marion, Allison Rutledge-Parisi, Michael Cadden, Drake Baer, Susan Kittenplan, David McDowell, Tom Cole, Olga and Chris Hartwell, Emery Snyder, Kim Benzel, Cynthia Walk,

Christopher Murray, Hans Homann, Alan Schrier, Dominic Balletta, Paul Eric Pape, Susan Lyons, Jeff LaHoste, David Clement, Peggy Wreen, Synthia Rogers, Linda Raya, Anne Poyner, Miss Lillian, the entire Wright family, and one used '86 Honda Civic named Madge that was once valued at almost twenty-five hundred bucks.

PORTRAIT OF AN ENIGMA

October, 1994. I have scoured my bathtub to a pristine white; my pencils have all been sharpened to lethal points. I have ground the coffee for the coming week, alphabetized my CD collection, and ironed my underwear. My loose change has been sorted and wrapped. I have sifted the cat litter, and answered phone calls dating back six months or more. I have no more excuses. It is time to write.

To ensure the speedy arrival of the Muse, I've erected a small shrine atop my desk. A toy Trabant, the notorious East German automobile, squats in front of me like a paperweight. A scrappy ceramic terrier, his ear cocked in perpetual alert, crouches next to my telephone. On the boom box near my computer, the great cabaret singer Hildegard Knef is belting out *"In Dieser Stadt."* My German dictionary lies at my side. Lining my bookshelves are pocket guides to Berlin, the short stories of Christopher Isherwood, dog-eared catalogs from a place called the *Gründerzeit* Museum, and encyclopedic volumes dedicated to antique furniture and daily life in the Third Reich. Yellowed postcards are tacked to the wall, and at my feet a tattered clump of paper; it's a Xerox copy of a Secret Police File. A framed portrait of my subject peers down from the wall, ready to bless and curse me as I mold her life into a play. With these artfully arranged knickknacks, I'm desperately trying to will inspiration into the room.

Still, no words come. My fingers hover, unmoving, over the keys.

Hours pass. Then years.

Back in the summer of 1992, my dear childhood friend John Marks alerted me to an astonishing subject for a play. At the time, he was bureau chief for *U.S. News and World Report* in Berlin, and—in the media's thirst for human interest stories following the fall of the wall—he had stumbled across a true eccentric in the local news: an elderly East German transvestite who lived in a rural suburb called Mahlsdorf about forty minutes outside the city.

Charlotte von Mahlsdorf, John told me, had lived openly as a cross-dresser under the twentieth century's two most conformist regimes—the Nazis and the Communists—for almost her entire life. Born Lothar Berfelde in 1928, she had long considered herself a member of the "third sex": a female spirit trapped in a male body. Hence her preference for female pronouns even before it became the politically correct mode of address for the transgendered. In addition to her sartorial quirks, Charlotte was a compulsive collector, a hoarder of history. In her mammoth stone mansion she housed a one-of-a-kind museum of curios, antiques, and bric-a-brac from the late nineteenth century. Perhaps most astonishingly, hidden in her basement, Charlotte had preserved the only surviving Weimar cabaret in all of Eastern Germany—an old tavern from the *Scheunenviertel* known as *The Mulack-Ritze*. For this effort she received the *Bundesverdienstkreuz*, or Order of Merit, from the Cultural Ministry following reunification.

As John recounted her story, I was mesmerized. I'd long

held a casual interest in gay history, and Charlotte seemed like a veritable treasure trove. There are only a handful of books about gay life in Germany during the Second World War, and even fewer about the plight of the homosexual under Communism. Charlotte's story, I reasoned, might help to fill in the considerable blanks. Furthermore, her quiet heroism—maintaining an unwavering sense of herself during such repressive times—could be a boon to gay men and women everywhere. In an age where politicians still routinely decry homosexuality on the evening news and "fag" remains the most stinging of all playground epithets, Charlotte's dogged insistence on her own sexuality could prove downright curative; an antidote for a community too often besieged by public condemnation and internalized self-loathing. She was a bona fide gay hero. If her life didn't merit two hours on a New York stage, I reasoned, whose would?

In a spasm of bravery I wrote Charlotte, asking her permission to visit. She granted it in a letter penned in baroque script on parchment paper. My first official trip was in January of 1993. Soon I was flying in and out of Tegel regularly. I'd take the rickety U-bahn ride out to Mahlsdorf with my cassette recorder in hand, my translator Jeffrey Schneider at my side, and a list of questions scrawled on a yellow legal pad. Each time I showed up at Charlotte's door, it would creak open, and she'd whisk us inside, down into the dusky basement where we'd sit in cane-backed chairs and talk into the wee hours of the morning. (Charlotte was a night owl, and rarely wanted to conduct our interviews before at least 10 p.m.) With a jar of yogurt in her hand, she would spill anecdotes and memories into my squawk box in her cadenced, almost singsong voice.

Meanwhile, Charlotte's fame throughout Germany was skyrocketing. She was profiled in magazines, and a frequent guest on talk shows. (Once, she appeared on a tabloid program with a dwarf, in a show dedicated to "celebrating difference!") She appeared in a documentary about her life by the maverick gay filmmaker Rosa von Praunheim, and even wrote her autobiography. As her trust in me grew, Charlotte let me accompany her on lecture tours. We would travel to tiny East German hamlets like Luckenwalde, and I would sit with the recorder running as the most unlikely fans imaginable—pig farmers and rubber tire magnates, bourgeois housewives and children—treated her with the respect of a visiting dignitary, fawning over her appearance and complimenting her signature pearls. Charlotte was so sweetly self-effacing, so coyly feminine, and so full of modest charm that even the hardcore locals forgave the fact that she was hiding a man's body beneath her pleats. Back in the United States, I'd transcribe my audiotapes dutifully into my computer. Over a two-year period, I had amassed over five hundred pages of transcript. In my giddy naïveté, I presumed the play would pour forth with relative ease.

But then something happened. Something so deeply unsettling it would cause my writerly imagination to freeze and prevent me from jotting a single word.

Like so many citizens of the East German state, Charlotte had a Stasi file, the confidential and incendiary report kept by the East German Secret Police. The document sat locked in a filing cabinet at the vast gray complex of offices known as the Ministry for State Security. After the collapse of Communism, Charlotte was allowed to apply for a copy, but it often took months, even years, to receive it because of the enormous backlog of requests. Foreign researchers with academic or press credentials could obtain the files with comparative speed. In a heart-stopping gesture, Charlotte cut a deal with me. If I would petition for her file and obtain it quickly, then I could keep a copy of my own. Together, ours would be the first civilian eyes to peruse its contents. (Later, the German press would discover it and cause a firestorm.)

To this day, I'm not sure why she gave the papers to me so willingly; perhaps she was simply overeager and wanted them too hastily. Perhaps she mistrusted my translation skills and presumed I'd never be able to actually read the file, or maybe she doubted my ability to piece together its dense, bureaucratic content. Another possibility was that she was seeking some kind of absolution and I was her chosen confessor.

The document was incriminating. Reputedly, in order to preserve her museum and maintain her idiosyncratic lifestyle, Charlotte had been more complicit with the Communist authorities than I ever dreamed. My gay hero had been a Soviet-sponsored spy.

I wanted my play to be a paean to Charlotte, but she was proving to be a much more complicated figure than I had ever imagined. Worse still, she had become a cherished friend; I loved her like a grandmother and I worried that the very act of writing a play about her might be tantamount to betrayal. The file claimed that she had willingly served as an informant, but—if I included that revelation in my play—was I merely informing on her?

I was further inhibited by the prospect of writing because—in order to capture the full measure of Charlotte's life—the script would have to span the entire twentieth century. I was daunted, too, by the challenge of accurately depicting realms of oppression that were firmly outside my experience. Nazis! Communists! As a privileged, white gay man from the ranch-style suburbs of Dallas, Texas, I couldn't claim any authority on subjects that enormous, that brutal. I'd barely made it through William L. Shirer's epic tome *The Rise and Fall of the Third Reich*, and I knew next to nothing about life at the Kremlin at the height of the Cold War. In the face of history so vast, I was an ill-informed pipsqueak, an intellectual rube.

And so I became paralyzed; unable to write a word, staring dumbly at my blank computer screen for six long years, souvenir curios strewn across my desk like so many impotent talismans. I'd complete other projects during that time—a play about the Marquis de Sade called *Quills* and its subsequent screenplay—but Charlotte was relegated to the bottom drawer.

Finally—in the spring of 2000—the dam burst. I was at a writer's retreat in Ucross, Wyoming; nothing but vast sky, cattle, and time to scribe. The retreat's artistic director, Robert Blacker, and I were engrossed in conversation over chocolate chip cookies and milk. I was feebly defending my writer's block. "I just can't do it, Robert," I moaned. "I can't write this play. My subject exceeds me."

Robert exploded. "You're right!" he cried. "You have absolutely no authority—moral or academic—to write about twentieth-century Europe! No credibility whatsoever!" He sat back in his chair, his eyes penetrating mine. "You're an authority on one subject, and one subject alone: *your ongoing obsession with a remarkable character*."

I felt a chill along my spine.

"Your passion for her, your disillusionment—it has all the makings of a romance," he continued. "Whatever you do, don't write a play about history. Write a play about your love affair with Charlotte von Mahlsdorf. If you're lucky, the requisite history will take care of itself."

It was the most liberating gift a fellow artist could give; permission to write my own story. For the first time, the play's structure dawned on me. It wouldn't be a straightforward biographical drama; it would chart my own relationship with my heroine. I would even appear as a character, a kind of detective searching for Charlotte's true self.

At first, the notion appalled me: depicting myself onstage? It felt like the most flagrant act of narcissism a writer could commit. Furthermore, I was a playwright, not a memoirist; I hid my true self behind invented characters far more colorful and articulate than I. Nevertheless, the thematic possibilities seemed rich; if Charlotte were a curator of nineteenth-century antiquities, I would present myself in the play as a curator of her. The whole piece could be a rumination on the preservation of history: Who records it and why? What drives its documentation? Is it objective truth, or the personal motive of the historian? When past events are ambiguous, should the historian strive to posit definitive answers or leave uncertainty intact? The only way to pose these questions was through my own inclusion as a character. And if I were going to be presumptuous enough to parlay Charlotte's life as drama, how could I be bashful about my own? It would be hypocrisy of the most cowardly sort.

Enthused for the first time in years, I began to flip through my notes, and certain leitmotifs popped off the paper: Edison Amberols, my ever-growing stack of microcassettes, Charlotte's sepia photographs and aged diaries. Wasn't the whole play—at its core—about the process of recording?

I went back to my taped interviews with Charlotte and listened to them with renewed vigor. To my refreshed ear, her broken English suddenly constituted a remarkable kind of poetry. For example, a word in German for "to receive" is *bekommen*. In the past tense, Charlotte would say, *"Ich bekam diese Möbel"* or "I received this furniture." But when she translated that from German to English, she would say, "I became this furniture." How beautiful and true! I realized her own malaprop-ridden syntax was far better than any language I could invent on her behalf. I decided to compose the play largely from the interviews themselves.

Immediately, I felt a surge of guilt. I'd be hijacking a technique that the renowned director Moisés Kaufman had perfected with his play *The Laramie Project*. I'd known

Moisés for years; we'd spent time together at countless theater festivals across the country. How dare I appropriate his methodology! Then I thought, "My God, he's one of your dearest friends. Just ask the master to join you in the process."

That summer I was invited to work on the piece at the Sundance Theater Lab in Utah and I called Moisés, proposing that he direct. The story appealed to him immediately, because it possessed the two traits I think he relishes most: 1) a wildly compelling narrative, and 2) true sociological import. "Darling!" he exclaimed in his lilting Venezuelan accent, "a play about a transvestite; how theatrical!"

At the Lab—with my newfound director in tow to advise me—I could finally start fashioning a script. In addition, Sundance was willing to provide me with a cast of actors who could perform scenes as soon as the pages slid forth from the laser printer.

This induced another massive attack of guilt. Actors are expensive, especially for the workshop of an unwritten play. They have to be transported, housed, and fed, and they're a notoriously hungry lot. And the characters who populated Charlotte's life were legion; how many people would I need? The cast was potentially huge! "Just one actor to start," I told myself. "Someone to play Charlotte herself. Until the play truly locates its shape, it seems presumptuous to ask for more."

Instinctively, I rang up Jefferson Mays. He had appeared in the original production of my play *Quills* at the New York Theatre Workshop in the role of the priest, and gave a fearless, shockingly inventive performance. He was only too happy to leave a sweltering New York in July for the cool mountains of the Wild West, and soon the three of us— Moisés, Jefferson, and I—were on an airplane, headed for a month of immersion in all things Charlotte, my transcripts wedged in the overhead bin, and her Stasi file safely stowed under the seat in front of me.

A tiny cabin by a gurgling stream was our rehearsal hall. On the first day we convened, Moisés decided to employ some techniques he'd evolved with the Tectonic Theater Company. He asked me to pick out a few highlights from my voluminous notebooks—a favorite anecdote or a particularly telling interview exchange. I dutifully did so—a story about Charlotte's first dress, and another about her favorite gramophone—and I passed the pages to Jefferson. He started to read aloud.

At first, it was unnerving. With his startling gift for mimicry, he was transporting me back to Mahlsdorf, all the way to that notorious basement bar. Charlotte was thousands of miles away, but it felt as if she were truly in the room with us. In addition to Charlotte, Jefferson began to imitate other voices on the tape: my translator, even me.

I suddenly realized that I didn't need a bigger cast. In a play about a character that has to adopt a variety of guises in order to survive, it made sense to let one actor play all the roles. Furthermore, I loved the idea that Jefferson would inevitably be costumed in Charlotte's customary black dress and pearls, so every other character he played would, by default, also be wearing a little black dress. In our production, transvestism would be the norm, not the exception. Everyone from the callow playwright (me) to the fiercest Nazi officer would wear a skirt. How very democratic! Now I knew conclusively that *I Am My Own Wife* would be a one-woman show, performed by a man.

After a few days of scouring transcripts, I became dispirited again. A play is, after all, more than a series of interview exchanges: question, answer, question, answer, question, answer. Our work was feeling stagnant. Moisés knew he had to do something to break down the incapacitating wall I'd built between myself and my chosen subject. So he decided some lighthearted theatrical game-playing might do just the trick. He gave us all homework: that evening, we had to create small, two-minute sketches inspired by the transcripts we'd read.

The next day, like school children at show-and-tell, we performed our pieces for each other. Moisés went first. He draped a dress over a metal folding chair, and then, without uttering a word, very slowly—with the titillating deliberation of a striptease artist—he doffed his clothes. He stood in the breezy mountain air in nothing but boxer shorts and a mischievous gleam in his eye. Then, with incalculable grace, he slid one arm into the gown, then the next. In full, feminine glory, he smoothed his skirt, and smiled a smile of sheer transcendence. In some nether region between masculinity and femininity, he seemed to locate his true self. That was his presentation.

Next, I stood up and announced the title of my performance piece: "Charlotte Goes West." I cracked open a popular gay German guidebook called *Berlin von Hinten* (*Berlin from Behind*) and read descriptions of the various clubs and bars Charlotte had visited in those fateful weeks after the wall crumbled: a dive called Café Anal, with a papier-mâché waterfall and late-night drag shows; a bordello called Kumpelnest, boasting a clientele ranging from "post-punk to love-hungry gays!" Even a sauna called the Steam Club, famous for the adjustable air-jet nozzles in its Jacuzzi. With a satisfied blush, I sat down.

Jefferson performed last. With deceptive simplicity, he placed a shoe box on the table in the center of the room. Then, with an impish grin, he opened it, and plucked out a stunning homemade gramophone rendered in perfect miniature. He set it on the table. Next, he pulled out a tiny couch with felt cushions, then a grandfather clock. He'd stayed up into the wee hours, and crafted paper reproductions of Charlotte's beloved museum furniture, using shirt cardboard and a razor from his toiletry kit. Soon an entire room was arrayed before us like a dollhouse. My sense of theatrical possibility exploded, and I suddenly saw countless new ways of dramatizing my existing text. For the first time, the play started unspooling gloriously in my head.

I left Sundance with the show's first act, which dealt primarily with Charlotte's life during World War II. I'd been able to successfully avoid grappling with all the troubling information in her Stasi file. With palpable foreboding, I knew that material would have to figure prominently in the second act.

The following summer, Jefferson and I traveled to the La Jolla Playhouse near San Diego to further workshop the play; Moisés, who was directing a movie for HBO, was unable to join us.

As I sat under palm fronds in Southern California, poring over my smudged Xerox of Charlotte's file, I began to fret. When press reports had finally surfaced in Germany in 1997 about Charlotte's Stasi cooperation, they'd caused a furor. At the time, readers of her autobiography felt betrayed; why hadn't she disclosed the information in her own book? Gay men and women who had placed her on a pedestal were outraged; perhaps she wasn't such an effective poster girl, after all. And the general citizenry certainly didn't look too kindly on complicity. I feared that—if I included the detailed information contained in her file—my play might stoke the fires of outrage against her. Did I want to bear culpability for that?

Yet in my heart I knew that, despite my intentions to enshrine Charlotte, the Stasi file was a dramatist's goldmine. It made for a better play. To omit its content would render my central character benign: precious Trannie Granny, rescuing wartime artifacts, running her covert museum, and providing a role model for homosexuals everywhere. That's a character more suited to public relations than the rigors of drama. Dramatic heroines require dimension, the requisite character flaw that renders them human. I urgently needed to include Charlotte's duplicity; it was the price she paid for living the unequivocal, unapologetic life of a transvestite.

To suggest she accomplished something so bold without compromise was to minimize the achievement itself. True iconoclasm always comes at a price.

I renewed my research, scouring German periodicals and Web sites. Much to my relief, I soon learned that many of my dramaturgical fears had been outpaced by history and popular opinion. During the reunification process, the press learned that countless citizens had functioned as informants; it was almost commonplace. In the effort to reunify, the German people had no choice; they had to collectively forgive minor collaborators. The stigma, while still present, was markedly lessened. Animosity toward Charlotte had waned in the four years following those stinging newspaper reports, and—at long last—I felt permission to freely examine her own Stasi past. I could present Charlotte with all her haunting, vexing complexities intact and not damn her in the process.

Jefferson and I worked feverishly, and by the end of July 2001, I'd roughly shaped the entire play. Moisés took two days off filming to come and see a performance of our work so far. "Why, Douglas," he beamed, "I think you're onto something."

The three of us continued to travel across the country from theater to theater, honing the text in a series of workshops. At the Wilma Theater in Philadelphia, Jefferson performed the whole play with nothing but a music stand. At the About Face Theater Company in Chicago, we built an entire set, only to impulsively tear down three of its walls in a frenzy of inspiration. At the New York Theatre Workshop in Manhattan's East Village, the first act flew by, but the second sagged. Performance after performance, I would add new scenes and characters. (Some nights, Jefferson would have to fold three or four new accents into the show with nary a rehearsal.) Eventually—at our off-Broadway premiere at Playwrights Horizons—audiences confirmed our hunch; Charlotte von Mahlsdorf's life merited attention.

Unfortunately, Charlotte herself would never see a production. I had kept her apprised of the play's progress over the years, but regrettably she passed away in April of 2002. (When I got the news, I was thunderstruck. I had recently finalized plans to visit her at her new home in Sweden; the plane tickets were sitting in my bureau drawer. Instead, I'd find myself flying to Berlin for her memorial service.)

Further, though I was heartsick, there was a part of me that was also relieved. I'm often asked, "If she were still alive, what would she think of your script?" I can't answer for her. Nevertheless, I fervently hope—beneath the pages of transcript, the Stasi files, the old letters, and the newspaper articles that constitute the work—she'd see a love letter, peering out through all that paper.

As I write this, my slightly fictionalized Charlotte is preparing to make her Broadway debut. I have no idea how she'll fare in a venue that seems to favor Phantoms, smart-aleck puppets, and—lately—Mel Brooks. She doesn't have a chorus line or a knock-'em-dead eleven o'clock number—just a cunning smile and a few tantalizing secrets to share. I only pray she can cast the same enthralling spell over audiences at the Lyceum Theater as she did over me.

And that that spell will inspire others to continue excavating Charlotte's life. For although I dutifully set out to evoke the life of a real person, I have nevertheless taken the customary liberties of the dramatist. I have edited Charlotte's anecdotes for clarity; I have condensed several characters into one when it best served the drama of her story; I have created certain archetypal figures in the play, such as newspaper reporters, bureaucrats, and specialists; I have imagined certain scenes while wholly inventing others for narrative clarity and in pursuit of my own thematic purpose. While I hope the text does justice to the fundamental truths of Charlotte's singular life, it is not intended as definitive biography.

Hopefully, some day my play will be outdistanced by new revelations from scholars and critics far more expert than I, as it is my ardent wish that she move beyond the confines of the stage and into the pages of accredited history books.

Even at this late date, I'm still reluctant to call the play "finished." At the end of my long journey with Charlotte, I found she remained—at heart—an enigma. And how can you conclusively paint a portrait of that?

DOUG WRIGHT
October 2003

I AM MY OWN WIFE

I Am My Own Wife premiered on Broadway in a production by Delphi Productions and David Richenthat at the Lyceum Theater on December 3, 2003, following its Off-Broadway premiere at Playwrights Horizons, Inc. (Tim Sanford, artistic director), on May 27, 2003. It was directed by Moisés Kaufman; sets were designed by Derek McLane, costumes by Janice Pytel, lights by David Lander, and sound by Andre J. Pluess. The production stage manager was Andrea "Spook" Testani. The cast was as follows:

CHARLOTTE VON MAHLSDORF   *Jefferson Mays*

I Am My Own Wife was written with support from Playwrights Horizons, made possible in part by funds granted to the author through a program sponsored by Amblin Entertainment, Inc., and was developed in part with the support of the Sundance Theatre Laboratory. Workshop productions of the play were presented by La Jolla Playhouse (Des McAnuff, artistic director; Terrence Dwyer, managing director), and the About Face Theatre (Eric Rosen, artistic director), in association with the Museum of Contemporary Art, Chicago.

THE CAST

A single actor performs all of the roles in the play. Distinctions between characters are made by changes in the tonal quality and pitch of the actor's voice, and through his stance, his posture, and his repository of gestures. He glides fluidly from one personality to the next. Often his transformations are accomplished with lightning speed and minimal suggestion—a raised eyebrow, for example, or an unexpected smile.

THE COSTUME

His basic costume is deceptively simple. He wears a black skirt, rimmed with peasant piping at the hem, and a black blouse with short sleeves. There is a black kerchief on his head, and he has on sensible black walking shoes with scuffed toes. Around his neck is a delicate string of pearls. He wears no makeup.

His clothing is constant throughout most of the play. He rarely uses other costume pieces to represent fellow characters. This is his primary uniform.

The character of Alfred Kirschner is the one exception to this rule. At the top of Act Two, Alfred appears in an old plaid shirt, wool trousers, and a beret.

The dress designed by Janice Pytel for the original production of *I Am My Own Wife* was a marvel of versatility. It had the square shoulders of an officer's uniform and an almost masculine collar, but delicate pleats that tapered the torso in a feminine way. Without appearing overtly theatrical, the dress not only suited Charlotte herself but also subtly suggested the multitude of other characters in the play. The overskirt was full, so the actor could achieve a variety of effects by manipulating it artfully: raising it to marvel in the mirror as an awestruck young girl; lifting it to curtsy; coyly flipping it back and forth to flirt; and smoothing it with an old woman's modesty as she rises from a chair.

THE SETTING

A simple square room, indicated by floorboards and a rear wall, covered in delicate blue-gray lace. In the middle of the wall, a set of white French doors. Onstage, a plinth that will later hold Charlotte's beloved Edison phonograph. A table with four wooden chairs, carved in the neo-Gothic style. Beneath it, a large wooden box. Inside that box, doll furniture, accurately and lovingly carved.

For the original production of *I Am My Own Wife*, director Moisés Kaufman, set designer Derek McLane, and lighting designer David Lander worked in concert to create a heart-stopping effect on the rear wall of the theater. Looming behind Charlotte's modest quarters was a huge wall of shelving, overstuffed with antiquities: gilded mirrors, upturned chairs, ornate German cabinetry, porcelain dogs, sideboards, tea tables, music machines of all makes and varieties, old crystal chandeliers, bureaus, bric-a-brac, and bronze busts—marvelous debris culled from the nineteenth century and hoarded with a kind of obsessive grandeur. At key moments in the text, nine or ten gramophone horns would suddenly erupt in light, revealing themselves for—seemingly—the first time. At other times, twenty clocks would ignite and chime. When Charlotte descended into the famous old cabaret—*die Mulack-Ritze*—countless tiny, fringed lamps with red bulbs sprang to life. The wall gave the play an epic scope; Charlotte's repeated descriptions of furniture became—through visual enhancement—a record of lives lived through the objects that were left behind. At the same time, this wall was used with such prudence that visual pyrotechnics were never allowed to upstage the content of Charlotte's own remarkable stories.

These ingenious flourishes belong to the play's original creative team, but I hope they suggest the magical possibilities of Charlotte's world.

CHARACTERS

(in order of appearance)

CHARLOTTE VON MAHLSDORF

JOHN MARKS

DOUG WRIGHT

TANTE LUISE

SS OFFICER

SS COMMANDER

YOUNG LOTHAR BERFELDE

HERR BERFELDE

PRISON GUARD

MINNA MAHLICH

CULTURAL MINISTER

STASI OFFICIAL

ALFRED KIRSCHNER

YOUNG HOMOSEXUAL MAN

AMERICAN SOLDIER AND HIS BUDDY

CUSTOMS OFFICIAL

STASI AGENT

PRISON OFFICIAL

NURSE

GERMAN NEWS ANCHOR

POLITICIAN MARKUS KAUFMANN

ULRIKE LIPTSCH

JOSEF RÜDIGER

ZIGGY FLUSS

FIRST NEO-NAZI

SECOND NEO-NAZI

BRIGITTE KLENSCH

KARL HENNING

FRANÇOIS GARNIER

SHIRLEY BLACKER

DAISUKE YAMAGISHI

MARK FINLEY

PRADEEP GUPTA

CLIVE TWIMBLEY

DIETER JORGENSEN

ACT ONE

(The French doors at the rear of the room open, and standing before us is CHARLOTTE VON MAHLSDORF.

She is, in fact, a man, roughly sixty-five years old. CHARLOTTE *wears a simple black housedress with peasant stitching, a kerchief on her head, and an elegant strand of pearls.*

She gazes at the audience for a moment; the tiniest flicker of a smile dances on her lips. Then, surprisingly, she closes the doors as quickly as she appeared, and is gone.

A pause. The stage is empty again.

In a moment, the doors reopen. CHARLOTTE *reappears. Cradled in her arms is a huge antique Edison phonograph, complete with an enormous horn in the shape of a flower. She grins, satisfied, and sets the phonograph on a small plinth.*

She steps back for a moment to admire the music machine. When she speaks, it's in broken English, but the

cadences of her voice are delicate; there's a musical lilt to
her inflection. She has a German accent.)

A LECTURE ON THE PHONOGRAPH

CHARLOTTE: Thomas Alva Edison was the inventor of the first
talking machine of the world, in July of 1877. And, you see,
the record is not *ein Plattenspieler; nein*. It is a cylinder
made of wax. And this record is working with a hundred and
sixty revolutions per minute, and is playing four minutes
long. And the record is made by the National Phonograph
Company in Orange, New Jersey. At one time, I had over
fünfzehntausend cylinders.

*(CHARLOTTE indicates a painting of the Edison
phonograph with an attendant dog, its ears cocked to
listen.)*

And you see on the wall a painting: the dog Nipper, *His
Master's Voice*. The most famous trademark in all the world.
Next month, this phonograph will be half a century old.

*(She begins to turn the handle on the phonograph,
readying it for play.)*

For fifty years, I've been turning its crank.
The loudness depends on a big or a small horn. Metal
horns are better for bands and the voices of men. And the

wooden horns, they are better for the strings and the voices of the female. *Die Sopranistin.* And Edison's phonograph has in the needle a little sapphire.

(She plucks a tiny disposable needle from a drawer concealed in the phonograph. She holds it up to the light, and says emphatically):

Nicht Diamant, nur Saphir. And when it grazes the record it sounds so nice.

(She installs the needle on the arm, then delicately places the arm on the wax cylinder. The machine begins to play—an old German waltz, scratchy and exquisite.)

In the Second World War, when the airplanes flew over Mahlsdorf, and the bombs were coming down, I played British and American records. And I thought, They can hear in the airplanes that I am playing Edison records. I thought, If they hear me they will know I'm their friend.

(A pause as CHARLOTTE *revels in the music.*

Then—abruptly—the music stops. CHARLOTTE *is supplanted by someone else, a thirty-something newsman named* JOHN MARKS.

JOHN *has the intrepid spirit of a Saturday serial matinee hero. His voice has a Texas twang. His masculine edge stands in sharp contrast to* CHARLOTTE*'s demure nature.)*

THE WORLD FLIPS UPSIDE DOWN

JOHN:
From the desk of John Marks
Bureau Chief, Berlin
U.S. News & World Report
September, 1990.

Dear Doug,

It's a funhouse over here. You can't imagine. The Berlin Wall falls and the world flips upside down.

All the great and powerful leaders are turning out to be clowns. Erich Honecker, one of the most feared and respected dictators in the world, has in one year become a fugitive. He wanders around the grounds of a Soviet military hospital in his pajamas. Secret police files kept on East Germans for four decades are being released, and it turns out husbands spied on their wives, children on their parents, dissidents on each other.

(He steps forward, and adopts a more confidential tone.)

Now, in the midst of all this craziness, I've found a true character; she's way up your alley. (And, believe me, I use the term "she" loosely.) I'd love to interview her—make her my first official article for *U.S. News & World Report.* But I'm afraid my editor will say her story's too extreme. Still, I think she may well be the most singular, eccentric individual the Cold War ever birthed.

Have I piqued your interest?

Love,
John

(Another abrupt shift. DOUG *is a playwright, in his mid-thirties, with an eager-to-please manner and a somewhat mellifluous voice.)*

DOUG: "Piqued" indeed.

August 8, 1992. I've been in Berlin for two days now. I'm sleeping on John's floor. Today we went to the Reichstag. There were demonstrations, because Cristo wants to cover it in pink tulle. Now we're in John's car, headed toward the east.

*(*DOUG *glances out an invisible window, as though he were riding in a car with* JOHN.*)*

Through the windshield, I can see fragments of the infamous wall still standing. Slapped onto one in bold paint are the words "Art Survives."

A sign whizzes past: "Mahlsdorf." It's a grim place; vast

apartment complexes rise like cement gulags. Then we turn a corner, and it's like we've turned back the clock two hundred years or more. Standing before us is a huge, weather-beaten mansion made entirely of stone. About a hundred tourists are gathered at the front door. Suddenly, with a creak, it opens.

(DOUG *morphs into* CHARLOTTE. *She fingers her pearls. Music from an Edison Amberol wafts through the air.*)

DAS GRÜNDERZEIT MUSEUM

CHARLOTTE: *Wilkommen in meinem Gründerzeit-Museum.* Welcome to my Gründerzeit Museum.

Here, people can always come to see my collection. Everything from *die Gründerzeit*; this was the period in Germany between 1890 and 1900. *Wie soll ich sagen . . .* "the Gay Nineties." Petroleum lamps and vases, gramophones, records, matchboxes, telephones, ink wells, Polyphones, pictures, credenzas, bureaus, and, of course, clocks.

No matter what people want to see or hear, I'll show or play it. Some people, they come to see me. *Ich bin Transvestit.* But soon they look at the furniture.

Folgen Sie mir bitte, ja?

(CHARLOTTE *pulls the doors of the museum open.*)

CHARLOTTE: This old door? It is not original, *nein.* I saved it from a house on Prenzlauer Street. Before the Russians blew up the houses, I took such things.

(As CHARLOTTE *enters the museum,* DOUG *addresses the audience directly, recounting the adventurous step into the unknown.)*

DOUG: She ushers us into the foyer of the museum. The ceilings are high, at least fifteen feet. We're huddled together like schoolchildren. For the next two hours—room by room, object by object—she guides us through the house.

*(*CHARLOTTE *seats herself at a small, ornately carved wooden table. From beneath it she pulls a velvet jewelry box. She places it squarely in the center of the table. With great ceremony, she opens it.)*

CHARLOTTE: Come in, please. There is room for everyone, yes?

*(*CHARLOTTE *pulls a small, lovingly carved, elegantly furnished doll dresser from the box. She holds it sweetly in her palm and approaches the audience, holding it out for inspection.)*

CHARLOTTE: Here we have *eine alte Anrichte.* A cupboard, yes? *Und dieses Möbelstück* is made of oak, in the style of neo-Renaissance. But this was not handmade; this was factory-made. So-called mass production. And the trim? People would tear it off; they would burn it. They did not like the scalloped wood, the tiny turrets, the ornamental molding. "Too old-fashioned! Too difficult to dust!" But me . . . I had a feeling for such things. And so I saved it.

(She removes a tiny lacquer cabinet of lighter wood.)

Und hier haben wir ein Vertiko. An old sideboard, *ja?* It was designed and built by *ein Tischlermeister*, Otto Vertiko, in *achtzehnhundertfünfundneunzig.*

(She pulls out a tiny bust on a pedestal.)

And this is a bust of Wilhelm II, the last German emperor. During the Second World War, they wanted to melt it down for munitions. And so—with my school friend Christian—I pulled it from the bonfire, yes? It looks like a bronze bust, but it is only zinc. Galvanized. Not so expensive.

(Next, a miniature clock with an open, suspended pendulum.)

In French, this clock is called *"regulatour."* Because it is regulating the time. And *auf Deutsch* we say *"Wanduhr," oder "Freischwinger."* Because the pendulum isn't encased in a glass box; it's freely suspended. Of course, American soldiers thought they were nice. They didn't have them in the USA. It made a nice gift to bring to the little wife at home, *ja*?

To wind such a clock, you need a key. And I collected, when I was a child, many keys. Keys for desks. Keys for doors. Keys with no locks; castaways. These I still carry in my apron, *ja*?

(She extracts a tiny gramophone.)

And here we have an old gramophone. *Nicht* phonograph, *Sondern* gramophone. Instead of cylinders, round plates, flat, *mit* grooves. At one time I had many such records— Mendelssohn and Offenbach. But during the time of Hitler it was very dangerous to possess music from Jewish composers. And so I thought, I must save these records. And so I took old paper—brown grocery paper—and I cut it in the shape of labels. And I wrote with ink false titles: Aryan polkas and waltzes, yes? And I glued them onto the records, for safety. And when the war was over I took a sponge and with water I took the labels back off. And then the Hebrew titles with the dog Nipper were visible again.

(A dainty little kitchen contraption, affixed to the edge of a tiny cutting table.)

The kitchen is as it was for a housewife of 1890 in Berlin. This machine is for pitting the stones of cherries.

(She regards the tiny room—now spread out before her on the table, like the parlor in a dollhouse—for a moment.)

When families died, I became this furniture. When the Jews were deported in the Second World War, I became it. When citizens were burned out of their homes by the Communists, I became it. After the coming of the wall, when the old mansion houses were destroyed to create the people's architecture, I became it.

(A pause, and then):

I am like a maidservant in this house; you must clean and clean, because the dust is growing! And the dust is looking like the dust of 1890! And you must put it away! I worked thirteen years with two hands to repair this old house. Each tile on the roof, I know. Each plank of the floor, like an old lover. In August 1993, the collection exists at the museum in this house for thirty-three years.

(She holds up a small collection box.)

And now you may make *eine Spende*. A small contribution. We have a cash box. Each person, what he or she thinks.

(She curtsies, then transforms into DOUG.*)*

POPPING THE QUESTION

DOUG:
From the desk of Doug Wright
New York City

Dear Charlotte von Mahlsdorf,

Recently, while in Berlin, I visited your museum. My childhood friend John Marks and I were awestruck by your furniture collection and your astounding array of Edison phonographs.

But I must confess, I was no less impressed by the mere fact of your survival. I grew up gay in the Bible Belt; I can only begin to imagine what it must have been like during the Third Reich.

The Nazis, and then the Communists? It seems to me you're an impossibility. You shouldn't even exist. So here's the presumptuous portion of my letter. I would love the opportunity to continue to study your life in order to write a play about you. With your support, I can apply for funding, fly back to Berlin, and begin to write in earnest. As far as grant applications go— forgive me—but from where I sit, you're a slam dunk.

Even if you reject my proposal, please know that the morning you shared with us was one of the most memorable of my life. Thank you for your kind attention, and I look forward to hearing from you.

Sincerely,
Doug Wright

(CHARLOTTE *puts the letter down; she pauses, considering the request.*)

CHARLOTTE:
Dear Mr. Wright,
   Yes. Perhaps it is possible for you to make a play. Maybe you will visit Berlin after Christmas.

Sincerely,
Charlotte von Mahlsdorf

(DOUG, *ecstatic, springs into action, giving the thumbs-up sign; they're in business now! He circles the stage, reciting into his mini recorder.*)

DOUG: Testing. Testing one-two-three. Testing.
   Tape One. It's January 20, 1993. I'm headed to the Gründerzeit Museum in Mahlsdorf for my first official interview with Charlotte von Mahlsdorf. With me, John Marks.

(*He sits. On one side, presumably, is* JOHN MARKS. *On the other,* CHARLOTTE.)

TRANSLATING TANTE LUISE

DOUG: John—if you could, please—would you ask Charlotte about her given name? Her legal name?

JOHN: *(his Texas twang evident) Was war Ihr Geburtsname?*

CHARLOTTE: *Mein Geburtsname war Lothar. Lothar Berfelde.*

JOHN: It was Lothar—

DOUG: Yeah, yeah. I got that. And next, could you ask her when she knew . . . the precise time . . . that her name ought to be Charlotte?

JOHN: *(even sharper on the ear this time) Und wann wussten Sie, dass Ihr Name Charlotte hätte sein sollen?*

(CHARLOTTE decides to put an end to this auditory torture.)

CHARLOTTE: I can tell it in English, yes?

(JOHN and DOUG exchange a look. CHARLOTTE takes over the telling of the tale.)

CHARLOTTE: *Meine* Tante Luise was working on an estate in East Prussia, and she raised horses. On a large farm. And since she was fifteen years old she never wore ladies' clothes. No.

Only boots. And jodhpurs. The clothes of a land inspector, and not a fine lady.

(She gives a long, knowing look to punctuate that thought. Then she continues.)

And so I was coming in August in 1943 to East Prussia and I found in her closet clothes. Girl's clothes. And . . .

(She whispers with an almost erotic intensity.)

. . . I . . . put . . . them . . . on.

(CHARLOTTE steps before an imaginary mirror. She gazes into it as if she were looking at herself—truly examining herself—for the first time. And she's delighted by her image in the glass. She turns, raising her skirt as if it were an exotic fan.

Suddenly she's stricken with a look of terror. She sees another reflection, looming behind her.)

And my aunt was coming into the room, and I was standing there, and she looked at us in the mirror, and then she said:

(CHARLOTTE becomes TANTE LUISE, with a stirring alto voice.)

TANTE LUISE: *Weisst du, mit uns beiden hat die Natur sich einen Scherz erlaubt. Du hättest ein Madchen werden müssen und ich ein Mann!*

(She repeats the phrase—eloquently—in English.)

Did you know that nature has dared to play a joke on us? You should've been born a girl, and I should've been a man!

(TANTE LUISE *morphs back into* CHARLOTTE.)

CHARLOTTE: And there was—on the bookshelf—a book. And *meine* Tante took this book down and handed it to me. The binding, it was blue. And I opened it. And on its *Titelbild*— "frontispiece"—*"Die Transvestiten, by Magnus Hirschfeld." Und ich spürte eine Gänsehaut . . . über meinen Rücken kriechen.* I felt a shiver down my spine. And *meine* Tante Luise said, "Read."

(CHARLOTTE *begins to read.*)

In each person, there is a delicate balance of male and female substances. Just as we can't find two matching leaves from the same tree, it is scientifically impossible to find two human beings whose male and female characteristics match in kind and number.

(*She passes the book to* DOUG.)

CHARLOTTE: (*to* DOUG) Read.

(*Now he reads from the text.*)

DOUG: *And so we must treat sexual intermediaries—those individuals who defy the ready classification of "man" or "woman"—as a common . . . utterly natural . . . phenomenon?*

(He looks to CHARLOTTE *for approval; she nods and says):*

CHARLOTTE: Yes. And *meine* Tante said:

TANTE LUISE: This book is not just any book. This book, it will be your Bible.

CHARLOTTE: *(to* DOUG, *lightheartedly) Möchten Sie ein paar Spritzekuchen?*

*(*DOUG *ducks aside, his invisible tape recorder primed, and makes a few private observations.)*

THE GIVEAWAY

DOUG: Charlotte's just slipped into the kitchen, to bring us some *Kaffee und Kuchen.* I brought a camera, but I'm too shy to ask her to pose . . . I'm afraid she'll think I've only come to gawk. So I wanted to record a quick . . . visual . . . an impression.

She's about five eight, maybe a hundred and seventy pounds. Sixty-five years old. Doesn't look like a drag queen *at all.* No makeup. I asked her about that; she says she "doesn't need it." She's got piercing eyes—really smart eyes—and a sly little crooked smile. She still wears her own hair, which is white, goose-feather white, cut in—I guess you'd call it a pageboy. She's got on a black peasant dress, a string of pearls, and heavy black shoes. Orthopedic shoes.

She doesn't have breasts—not really—but just enough paunch to sort of enhance the impression.

But her hands are big, and thick. The hands of a woodworker. A craftsman. Definitely a man's hands.

(DOUG *raises his own hands as if they belonged to* CHARLOTTE. *As he does so, he transforms back into her.*

CHARLOTTE *puts another Edison Amberol on the phonograph, and the room fills with the sound of nostalgia.*)

ARE YOU A BOY OR A GIRL?

CHARLOTTE: And the last days of the world war were the most dangerous time for me because I refused to carry a weapon or to wear a uniform. Instead, I had my hair long and blond and my mother's coat, and the shoes of a girl. And so I was—in Germany we say *"Freiwild."* Like the Jews, we were wild game.

Berlin was destroyed. I was walking about—the houses were all broken—and the street was full of rubble. Yes. And I would turn a street, and there was coming Russian airplanes with the splatter bombs—so close you could see the pilot with the helmet and the goggles. And this was very dangerous, because wherever you were standing the splatter bombs exploded into the earth. Pieces went everywhere. There was no escape.

And there was—on the corner—standing an air-raid shelter. And so I went inside. And I was sitting there maybe half an hour.

And I could hear the bombs, and the old building was shaking. And suddenly the door opened, and in came four SS officers. Infantry police. *Die Kettenhunde.*

And they were looking for boys and men and old men which were hiding, without weapons. And so they dragged me up to the police station. And I had to stand outside against the wall.

The SS men were standing four, maybe five meters away.

(She becomes the SS OFFICER, *and plays out the scene in real time.)*

SS OFFICER: *(doctrinaire)* All deserters shall be shot.
CHARLOTTE: And they wanted to shoot me. I looked down—I didn't want to see them shoot. I thought, I'll wait until I feel it. But when I looked to the ground I saw the boots of a commander.

(Her gaze rises as she sizes up the COMMANDER *with both awe and dread.)*

And he looked at me.
SS COMMANDER: Are you a boy or a girl?

CHARLOTTE: And I thought, If they shoot me, what's the difference between à boy and a girl, because dead is dead!

(She becomes a child and answers.)

YOUNG LOTHAR: I am a boy.

SS COMMANDER: How old are you, then?

YOUNG LOTHAR: Sixteen.

CHARLOTTE: And he turned around to face the execution squad commander.

SS COMMANDER: *(with some measure of self-contempt)* We are not so far gone that we have to shoot schoolchildren.

CHARLOTTE: And this was my salvation.

(CHARLOTTE lifts the needle off the wax roll and becomes DOUG.)

LISTENING

DOUG:

My dear Charlotte,

Enclosed please find two antique cylinders. Your favorite: John Philip Sousa. *El Capitan* and *Semper Fidelis*. They're Blue Amberols, so you should be able to play them on your Edison Standard.

I, meanwhile, am listening to our interview tapes every chance I get. On the treadmill. In the car. I've also started reading the works of Magnus Hirschfeld, and studying

German history since the time of Wilhelm II. Still, all I can think about is the story of your life.

(Then, with feeling):

You are teaching me a history I never knew I had. Thank you.

(a pause)

Tape Seven. January 26, 1993.
CHARLOTTE: *Heute habe ich einen Spitznamen fur dich.*
DOUG: A nickname? For me?
CHARLOTTE: "Thomas Alva Edison."

*(*CHARLOTTE *smiles inscrutably, then sits.)*

You have a talking machine, too, yes? Only his was made of tinfoil with a tiny stylus, and yours . . . yours is a . . .

(She leans in to read the inscription on DOUG's *tape recorder.)*

. . . "Sony Microcassette Recorder with voice activation and automatic playback." Hmm.
DOUG: *(grinning)* Charlotte's boyhood. Continued from previous tape.

*(*CHARLOTTE *begins to speak.)*

VATERLAND

CHARLOTTE: When I was a baby and then a little child—

DOUG: Can I interrupt you for a moment, and play that back?
I'm not sure—the batteries—

CHARLOTTE: Hmm. Yes, of course.

(DOUG futzes with the tape recorder.)

TAPE RECORDING: *(the voice of* CHARLOTTE*)* "When I was
a baby and then a little child—"

DOUG: We're good. Go ahead.

CHARLOTTE: My father was a Nazi.

(DOUG reacts.)

And he was brutal. And he was for militarism. And the
years of marriage for my mother were a moratorium. My
mother, she wanted to *sich scheiden lassen*. Get a divorce.
And my aunt said one day to me:

TANTE LUISE: If your father beats your mother once more,
she could die.

CHARLOTTE: And it was luck for us that in 1943 in Berlin the
government decreed the evacuation of mothers with children,
because of the air raids. And so my mother took the children
to East Prussia, to the house of my aunt. And at that time we
became good friends. Because my aunt was a lesbian, and I
was the same.

And one day I was cleaning the furniture, and I looked

through the window and it was snowing, and there was coming in the snow a man with a hat and a bag and I became horribly scared because I realized this was my father.

And my aunt and my father had a very heart discussion. And my aunt said:

TANTE LUISE: Your wife really wants a divorce from you.

CHARLOTTE: And suddenly my father pulled out a revolver, and pointed it at my aunt. And he said:

HERR BERFELDE: One more word and I'll shoot you.

CHARLOTTE: But my aunt took her revolver from the desk and said:

TANTE LUISE: I'll count to three, and then you better be out the door! Otherwise, *I'll* shoot.

CHARLOTTE: And she said:

TANTE LUISE: . . . *three!*

CHARLOTTE: *Und die Kugel durchschlug das Holz und blieb in der gegenüberliegenden Tür stecken*—the bullet went through one door and into the next, where it lodged, and my father returned to Berlin. And then I asked my aunt, and she said:

TANTE LUISE: Yes, of course. It's a shame I didn't kill him.

CHARLOTTE: Then, on the twenty-sixth of January 1945, my mother got a letter saying the government was taking over our house for Berliners who had lost their homes in the bombing. And so I went with the train to Berlin because I had to rearrange the furniture. To make room for the refugees.

(CHARLOTTE *seats herself at the table of antique models; it now suggests the house of her childhood, rendered in miniature. The scene seems to play out—doll-sized—in front of her.)*

And so I was coming into our house, and my father was living there, of course. And one evening, maybe it was the second or third day. No, I think it was a week—it was in the first week of February 1945—and one evening my father said to me:

HERR BERFELDE: This is the hour I ask you, Are you for me or your mother? Do you stand beside her or me?

CHARLOTTE: I was fifteen years old. And I asked him, "Aren't you ashamed of the way you've treated my mother?" And he said:

HERR BERFELDE: I'll shoot you down like a dog, and then I'll go to East Prussia and shoot your mother and your sister and your brother.

CHARLOTTE: And I thought of the words of my aunt. And I knew that my father would do this.

He locked me in the bedroom by turning the key. Because it was war, I could hear the Allied bombs coming in the night. And then under the bed I saw a large wooden utensil used to mix cake—*wie sagt man*—a rolling pin. And I thought, I can take this as a weapon.

I wanted to sneak out the door, but it was tightly locked. But even then I had in my pocket . . . keys. So I very carefully opened the door, and I was going in the next room.

It was very dark, except for a little moonlight which was shining. And I saw my father. He was lying on the sofa in the dining room, and his gun lay on the chair next to him. And I saw the chair. I saw the pistol. And, in that moment, the clock—we had a Westminster clock—and the clock was chiming, and I saw my father's hand; he was reaching for his weapon. And in this moment I began beating him.

(She says with sudden ferocity):

   Eins! Zwei! Drei! Vier! Fünf!

(A pause. She dissociates herself for a moment, becoming oddly contemplative.)

   Hmm. *Yes.*
   And the next day the Criminal Police came. And they asked me for the motive. And I told them. And when I was arrested they brought me before the Youth Justice. And I was sentenced to the Youth Prison in Tegel. Four years' detention. And when they took me to the jail my mother was there. And we looked at each other in the eyes, and we knew that we were finally free from the monster.

*(*CHARLOTTE *bolts up from the table and becomes* DOUG, *frantically scribing a letter.)*

AUF DEUTSCH

DOUG: Oh, John!
I'm in way over my head. To kill: "*töten, tötete, hat getötet.*"
Christ, this language doesn't make any sense.

I'm still winding my way through *Die Transvestiten*. Sigh. In some sentences I can barely discern the verb. And the vocabulary I'm learning is . . . well . . . so *specific*. Yesterday in German class I made an ass of myself. The teacher told us to make "small talk." I froze, couldn't remember a single phrase. So I blurted out a few new words I'd translated the night before: "*Hi, ich bin Doug, und ich trage schwarze Spitzenunterwäsche.*" "Hi, my name's Doug, and I'm wearing black lace panties!"

The whole class just stared at me. Except for this one guy named Morris, who offered to take me shopping. Maybe I should try reading something else?

Love,
Doug

(Once again, DOUG *readies an interview tape for* CHARLOTTE.*)*

DURCH DIE LUFT

DOUG: Tape Nine. March 5, 1993.

*(*DOUG *practices a few innocuous lines of German.)*

"*Guten Abend,* Charlotte. *Und wie geht es* Dir *heute? Wie geht es* Ihnen *heute?*"

(He appears at CHARLOTTE's *door. He greets* CHARLOTTE *in her native tongue.)*

Guten Abend, Charlotte.

CHARLOTTE: *Guten Abend.*

DOUG: *Ich habe Deutsch gelernt, um Dein phantastisches Leben besser zu verstehen.*

CHARLOTTE: Excuse me?

DOUG: *Jetzt sollen wir Deutsch sprechen, ja?*

CHARLOTTE: You are learning to speak German?

DOUG: *Ein bisschen, ja. Ich habe mit Berlitz studiert.*

CHARLOTTE: You speak German. Me, English. I wear your clothes, and you wear mine.

DOUG: *Als das Ende des Kriegs kam, waren Sie noch im Gefängnis?*

CHARLOTTE: The Youth Penitentiary at Tegel? *Nein.* A miracle allowed me to escape, yes? I was serving my sentence, sitting on a cot brushing my hair with an old ivory comb from *meine* Tante. And I heard a guard cry in the hallway:

PRISON GUARD: The Russians! They're flying over our roof!

CHARLOTTE: And it was true! Soon the bombs began to fall! The walls, they toppled down like sand castles in the tide. And the guard cried, "Run!" And so I picked up my blanket and my alarm clock, and I ran. I ran. I ran. Through the iron gates. Past the ruins of the old Jewish synagogue. And I saw on the street the large Russian tanks. And behind the tanks were coming horses with painted wagons. The Allies were coming to Berlin. And then there came a coach with the officers! Decorated. Yes, yes. Russian soldiers, and they were giving loaves of bread to the people!

And it was spring! And the birds were singing in the trees! And it was an awful war.

EINE SPENDE

(A telephone rings: short, European tones. It rings again. And again.)

ANSWERING MACHINE: *(the voice of* JOHN*)* *"Sie haben die Wohnung von John Marks erreicht. Bitte hinterlassen Sie eine Nachricht nach dem Pfeifton."*
DOUG: Are you there? Hello? Anybody home?

(a protracted beep)

DOUG: . . . Christ, pick up, pick up, pick up . . .

*(*JOHN *picks up.)*

JOHN: *(groggy)* Huh?
DOUG: John?
JOHN: Doug?
DOUG: Listen, I've run out of grant money, so I'm canceling my May trip. But all is not lost—I've decided to sell my car.
JOHN: You ever heard of time zones? It's four fucking a.m.
DOUG: It's an '86 Honda Civic, and I think I can get about

three thousand dollars for it. That should finance at least a month overseas, maybe more—

JOHN: Whoa, whoa, whoa. You're gonna *sell your car*? Don't you think you're going a little loopy?

DOUG: *(a burst of frustration)* John! . . . *(impassioned)* Don't you see? She doesn't run a museum, she is one! The rarest artifact she has isn't a grandfather clock or a Biedermeier tallboy. It's her. *(in slow, measured tones)* So, please. If I come in June, can I still crash on your floor?

(A pause, and then DOUG *speaks into his recorder, triumphant.)*

Tape Fifteen. *June* 20, 1993.

*(*CHARLOTTE *smiles enigmatically, and gestures for* DOUG *to follow.)*

CHARLOTTE: Careful—you must watch the stairs. Today you follow me at your own risk. I show you *das Geheimnis*—the secret—of *meinem Gründerzeit Museum.*

*(*DOUG *obliges.)*

DOUG: *(into tape)* Charlotte's disappearing down a series of steps; I guess I'm supposed to go down after her. Christ, it's steep. Now we're in the basement, I think, of the house. It's dark. She's lighting a gas lamp.

(DOUG *looks about the room in wonder.*)

Holy shit. It's huge. Old-fashioned, rough-hewn tables on wrought-iron stands. Cane-back chairs. There's an enormous bar, made of oak, stocked high with glasses, liquors, and—it's porcelain, I can't quite tell, but it might be an ancient beer pump.

MULACK-RITZE

CHARLOTTE: Welcome to *die Mulack-Ritze.* An old tavern from the yesterday.

DOUG: The walls are mottled and old. Signs everywhere. There's one, written in thin script on yellowed paper:

CHARLOTTE: "Prostitution Is Strictly Forbidden! At Least, According to the Police."

DOUG: On a placard in bold type:

CHARLOTTE: *"Tanzen ist Verboten."* Dancing is forbidden. But we had this old phonograph—*mit einem Blumentrichter*—and we would dance in the back, *ja?*

A long time ago, this old bar was sitting in the barn district of Berlin on Mulackstrasse, number fifteen. From the time of the Emperor Wilhelm II, it was a restaurant for gays and lesbians. The owners wanted homosexuals because they didn't get drunk, they didn't fight, and they always had money to pay for the bill.

At this very table *haben* Bertolt Brecht, Marlene Dietrich, the sexologist Magnus Hirschfeld, *und* the actress Henny Porten *alle gesessen, ja?* This table, he is over one hundred years old. If I could, I would take an old gramphone needle and run it along the surface of the wood. To hear the music of the voices. All that was said.

Minna Mahlich, she was the barmaid, *ja?* And in 1963 she came to me and she said:

MINNA MAHLICH: The *Kommunisten*, they want to close us down. *Unsere Geschichte ist dekadent, ja?* Our history is decadent. We have only one day. And then the bulldozers.

CHARLOTTE: And I thought, That is not good.

So I bought this furniture—I paid a little bit of money— and I bought it for this museum here. Everything—every glass—is original, *ja?* I took it all with me here for safety and I hid it in *meinem Keller.* And the next day the Russians came, and the old bar on Mulackstrasse, they broke it down.

And then came the wall. And for us here in Eastern Berlin it was finished, gay life. The bars, closed. Personal advertisements in the newspaper, canceled. No place to meet but the tramway stations and the public toilets. We were not supposed to exist. *Persona non grata.*

So I thought to give homosexual women and men community in this house. Yes. It was a museum for all people, but I thought, Why not for homosexuals?

So we met here—in *die Mulack-Ritze*—on the Sunday afternoons. And sometimes in front of the crowd Minna would run a finger along the bar, and when it came up black with dust, she'd cry:

MINNA MAHLICH: Charlotte, you pig! You haven't cleaned!

CHARLOTTE: And I'd tell the visitors, "This is a historic moment! This is Minna Mahlich, the last owner of the Mulack-Ritze." And the people would all clap and laugh.

And there was over the bar an attic. When a boy or girl met a man, and wanted to go upstairs, they could. Two men, two girls, a boy and a girl—it didn't matter. And they'd go into this room. A divan, a sofa, a chaise longue, a bed. A screen separated each space. Every piece of furniture was always in use. A pair in every free seat!

And anyone with an interest in sadomasochism, whether it was two or four or six, could have the room to themselves for a few hours. Whips and things to beat on the behind.

And the Stasi—the Communist secret police, the most feared government spies of all the world—was coming, and they were looking in the windows, and they were saying, "What's this?" So what could I do? I painted all the windows black.

(DOUG *speaks reverently—in hushed tones—into his own recorder.)*

DOUG: When the wall falls, Charlotte tells me—she had the only surviving Weimar cabaret in all of Eastern Germany. Hidden in the basement of her house in Mahlsdorf. Which she ran—under the watchful eye of the Stasi—for almost thirty years.

(Suddenly, a blast of pompous music.

The MINISTER OF CULTURAL AFFAIRS *approaches the podium to make a speech.)*

BUNDESVERDIENSTKREUZ

CULTURAL MINISTER: On behalf of the Cultural Ministry of the *Bundesrepublik Deutschland*, it gives me great joy and honor, in recognition of your astonishing efforts at conservation, your steadfast preservation of a noted period in German industrial design—

*(*CHARLOTTE *intercedes, to ensure that he says it correctly.)*

CHARLOTTE: *Die Gründerzeit.*
CULTURAL MINISTER: *(utterly charmed by* CHARLOTTE*)*— *die Gründerzeit,* and your timely rescue of the Mulack-Ritze, to offer you membership in the high order of the *Bundesrepublik Deutschland* and deliver unto you the Medal of Honor—a cross upon a ribbon.

(The music amps, followed by thunderous applause and cheers. CHARLOTTE *curtsies. The sound fades.)*

CHARLOTTE: The day I received the medal was for me recognition of my work, and I thought—*wie soll ich sagen*— I thought, It's good, because other people see that a transvestite can work. A transvestite becomes such a medal!

If other people—heterosexual people—they look at the
television, and they read the newspapers and they say, "Ah!
He or she is able to work, *ja*."

JOHN: They presented the award on national German
television. Aw, Doug, I wish you could've been there. Picture
it. An elderly man, in a skirt and a string of pearls. Nobody
laughed. No catcalls. And, at the end of the ceremony, the
Cultural Minister himself even leaned down to kiss her hand.

BERLIN FROM BEHIND

DOUG: *(to* CHARLOTTE*)* Charlotte, what was it like? To visit
the West after the wall came down?

*(A sudden blast of music; it's cheesy German disco, a
song called "Super Paradise."*

CHARLOTTE *smooths the creases in her skirt and plucks a
small guidebook called* Berlin von Hinten *from the table. A
few well-placed steps across the stage, and she has crossed
the border into Western Berlin.*

*She reaches a particular address, and admires the facade
of an imagined building. She consults her guidebook,
and reads aloud.)*

CHARLOTTE: "Café Anal. The crowd is gay and lesbian, leftist
punks and muesli freaks. Sunday night is two-for-one beer

blast. Other events include gay slide shows about South America, karaoke, and drag-queen bingo!"

(CHARLOTTE *raises an eyebrow, then moves on, dancing ever so slightly to the throbbing beat.*)

"Buddy's Bar. The dignified ambience of black leather is enhanced with hot music and stimulating porn videos, and a young boy can usually be persuaded to give a little show."

(CHARLOTTE *folds down the corner of the page; this pub is definitely worth remembering.*

A final stop on her whirlwind tour.)

"Prinz Eisenherz Buchladen. This gay bookstore stocks everything ever written by homophiles, nancies, pansies, sissies, trannies, sodomites, Sapphists, fruitcakes, homos, faggots, lezzies, dykes, queens, queers, gender-benders, and friends of Dorothy."

(CHARLOTTE *balks.*)

CHARLOTTE: *(muttering to herself)* I don't know what that means . . .

(*The music stops.* DOUG *asks, in measured tones*):

DOUG: Now, Charlotte, I heard in the seventies the Stasi came to you, and offered to treat you very well if you would give the names and addresses of the people who frequented your museum. I heard they actually promised you a car. Is that right?

I, LOTHAR BERFELDE

(CHARLOTTE's *demeanor changes; she speaks cautiously.*)

CHARLOTTE: Yes. And one day they came, and one of the two men said to me:
STASI OFFICIAL: You have to sit down. Take a paper and a pencil, and I will dictate to you the following . . .
CHARLOTTE: *(suspiciously)* And I thought, What's that?
DOUG: *(with certainty)* So you didn't do it?
CHARLOTTE: *(indignant)* He wanted me to write exactly what he said!
DOUG: *(with apprehension)* And what was the text you were expected to write?

(CHARLOTTE *picks up a slip of paper from the table; she reads haltingly.*)

CHARLOTTE: "I, Lothar Berfelde, commit myself willingly and freely to working together with the Ministry for State Security. I will report all information which may have the character of an action inimical to the state."

(She pauses. It's difficult to continue, but she manages.)

"I will be known by the code name Park. I pledge to keep this secret even from my nearest friends and relatives."

(Another pause. She thinks of her mother. Of her siblings. Then—staunchly—to DOUG, *the end of the pledge.)*

"I have been informed that if I break this oath I will be prosecuted according to the laws of the GDR."
DOUG: *(hoping against hope)* And you had to sign it?
CHARLOTTE: *(quietly, definitively)* I signed it.

(Tension fills the room.)

And I said to myself, "I'll still do whatever I want." *Ich mache doch was ich will.*
DOUG: And then they left.
CHARLOTTE: *Ja, ja.*

(Another pause. CHARLOTTE *turns cagey.)*

Meine Tante Luise always said, "Be as smart as the snakes; it's in the Bible." She said, "Never forget that you are living in the lion's den. Sometimes, you must howl with the wolves."

*(*JOHN *bounds out of* CHARLOTTE's *chair.)*

BATED BREATH

JOHN: Doug. Listen up. *(beat)* The German press got its
hands on Charlotte's Stasi file. She was an informant, all right.
For four years, in the mid-seventies. It says she was "willing."
Even "enthusiastic." And that museum of hers? It was a drop-
off point for secret packages and documents of interest to the
Stasi. Charlotte reported on illegal antiques dealings. It even
says she was responsible for an arrest. A fellow collector. A
friend.

    The tabloids are having a field day. I've enclosed a few
clippings.

*(DOUG sifts through them, finding each new headline
more incredible than the last.)*

DOUG: "Charlotte von Mahlsdorf, Sexual Outlaw and Soviet
Spy?" *(beat)* "Mata Hari Was a Man: The Real Story of
Berlin's Most Notorious Transvestite." *(beat)* "Comrade
Charlotte: Is the Disguise She's Wearing More Than Just a
Dress?" *(beat)* John? I'll get back to Berlin just as soon as
I can.

*(Once again—from the phonograph—the mesmerizing lilt
of a German waltz. CHARLOTTE dances—a quiet little
reverie—all to herself.)*

HORNS

CHARLOTTE: Even when I was a little child, no one wanted phonographs. Everyone said to me, "It's so old-fashioned!" They all wanted radios. But what did I want with a radio? To hear Hitler babble? No, thank you! That is the reason that, even today, I don't have a radio or a television.

For me, gramophones, Polyphones, Pianolas—I must truly say—these machines gave me so much pleasure in my childhood. If I hadn't had them, I'm not sure I would've survived. Things were so ghastly with my father—everything my mother and I went through.

But the music would pour through the horn and make things better.

(And it carries her away, into some distant corner of her own mind.)

ACT TWO

*(In the darkness, the rollicking sound of an old Pianola.
Unexpectedly, it ends with the loud slam of a prison door.*

Lights rise on ALFRED KIRSCHNER, *lying on the floor of his
prison cell, striated by light. He looks a bit like a
cockroach that's been flipped on its back, helplessly.*

ALFRED's *prison uniform hangs on his thin bones like
sails on a mast. His glasses are thick, distorting his eyes.
His cap is woolen and patched. He has a caustic wit.
Slowly, he rises to a sitting position and addresses*
CHARLOTTE *as if she were the audience.)*

A LETTER FROM PRISON

ALFRED:
The 17th of April, 1972.

Dear Charlotte,
    I was dining at lunch, a scrumptious vegetable stew with
mashed potatoes—

(He bellows down the prison corridor to some unseen cook):

Truly exquisite!

(Then he turns back to CHARLOTTE *and resumes.)*

—when your note arrived. Today's the day I put aside to answer letters, and I thought, Well, if I don't get any mail today I'll just stop writing altogether. Then I'll die, lost and forgotten by the world. So it came in the nick of time. You urged me, "Don't give up! You're not forgotten! You never had hordes of friends, but so what? You always gave a little joy to people, and that's enough." What sweet sentiments, Charlotte. For your sake, I won't give up, and I'll live patiently for the day I'll be set free.

At night, I wrap myself in blankets. I still have headaches and dizzy spells, but I don't think it's the fault of prison conditions. I think it's just age. I've gone so blind I can barely read. I just wander from one doctor to the next. They zap you with electricity, record it on paper and—voilà—an electrocardiogram. The dentist here is a real dictator. He plans to pull another one of my teeth. By the time you get this letter, I'll probably be nothing but gums. Alfred sans teeth is not a pretty sight!

*(*ALFRED *curls his lips over his gums to appear toothless, and grimaces to illustrate his point.)*

Please give your family my warm regards. Tell them I'm
still the same old Alfred—-

(To a prison guard, somewhere in the darkness):

—and I won't be beaten down!

(Again, back to CHARLOTTE.*)*

When I'm released, I know exactly what I'll do. I'll play my
favorite old waltz on the piano. Strauss, probably. Then I'll
put *"Frühlingskinder"* on the Polyphone and play that,
too.

With a calliopic and symphonic farewell,
Your Alfred

*(*ALFRED *removes his glasses and becomes* DOUG. DOUG
stares at the glasses, considering them for a moment.)

ERASURE

DOUG:
Charlotte,
    I'm afraid—for me—your Stasi file is an exercise in
frustration.

(DOUG rests the glasses upside down on a nearby sideboard. As he speaks, he pulls off ALFRED's *beret. Beneath it is* CHARLOTTE's *black kerchief.)*

I've noticed repeated references to a fellow antiques collector; sometimes they use the word *Kunsthandler*. Other times, *Sammler*. But whenever his actual name appears, it's been blacked out. I turn the pages over, I hold them up to the light, and still I can't make it out.

(DOUG unbuttons ALFRED's *shirt to reveal* CHARLOTTE's *blouse and pearls. He lowers* ALFRED's *trousers, and under them is* CHARLOTTE's *pleated black skirt.)*

"Today, the informant Park had tea with BLANK. Park received a birthday card from BLANK. At 2:30 p.m. in the afternoon, Park telephoned BLANK."

(DOUG now stands in CHARLOTTE's *signature garb. He puts* ALFRED's *clothes in the sideboard.)*

I suspect BLANK was important to you. Otherwise, why would he merit inclusion in your file?
Please. Shed light, if you can.

(Delicately, CHARLOTTE *turns* ALFRED's *old glasses upright; he seems to stare out at her from a shelf on the sideboard. She considers him for a moment, fondly.)*

MYTHOLOGY

CHARLOTTE: I still have his birth certificate. Alfred Kirschner, born on the first of September, 1911.

We became friends because it was a rainy day. I was walking through the streets of Berlin, and I saw an antiquity shop. I had no money to buy old things, I only wanted to stay dry. As I strolled through the stock, I glanced around the corner, and I saw Alfred. He was looking at a Polyphone.

(She turns to ALFRED, *adopting both roles.)*

Do you own such a machine?

ALFRED: Of course. I'm a collector. I've been a collector since my childhood.

CHARLOTTE: I am a collector since my childhood, too!

ALFRED: Back at my house . . . just two or three blocks from here . . . I have about fifteen thousand records.

CHARLOTTE: *(flirtatiously)* Touché! I only have twelve thousand.

ALFRED: And where do you live?

CHARLOTTE: *(flouncing her skirts ever so slightly)* In Mahlsdorf. Across from the pig farm. Near the paper factory.

(She turns to us.)

With that, Alfred bought a few music boxes.

ALFRED: The weather is so awful today; why not pay me a

visit in Mulackstrasse? Mahlsdorf's a long way in this maelstrom.

CHARLOTTE: *(with recognition and delight)* Mulackstrasse? That's where you live?

ALFRED: What about it?

CHARLOTTE: Remember the old pub, the Mulack-Ritze? Now it's in my museum!

ALFRED: *(with a hint of seduction)* I've heard of your museum, and of you—but now I'm meeting you in the flesh . . .

CHARLOTTE: And so off we went to his apartment. He made some *Kaffee mit Schlag und Kuchen*. And we played a large Polyphone. And it wasn't long before he said:

ALFRED: Look in my private room.

CHARLOTTE: And I did. And there were records everywhere. Whole shelves. He had Caruso records. Comedians, dance orchestras, jazz, opera. Polyphones, gramophones, phonographs, juke boxes, symphonions, Pianolas, Spieldosen, orchestrions, Echophones, calliopes, Victrolas, Edison Standards, Amberols, paper rolls, hurdy-gurdies, organettes. Clocks, too. Wall clocks, mantel clocks, grandfather clocks, regulators by Lenzkirch and Gustav Becker, cuckoo clocks, alarm clocks, chronometers, and pocket watches. A breastplate from the Middle Ages. Of course, everybody knew that Alfred was homosexual. Later, I'd visit his house. Sometimes homosexual men were standing before his door, like prostitutes.

(A young man idles at ALFRED's stoop, insolently smoking a rolled cigarette.)

YOUNG HOMOSEXUAL MAN: You can't ring Alfred now. He has one man or two men with him. Just wait till he's ready, when he's done with his sexuality.

CHARLOTTE: No! I just came to swap gramophone records.

YOUNG HOMOSEXUAL MAN: Oh, you're a transvestite!

CHARLOTTE: And how they cackled until Alfred opened the door to let me in.

(CHARLOTTE *steps into a focused pool of light, adopting the role of narrator in the upcoming tale.*)

One day Alfred bought a clock from a local antiques dealer. He was headed home down Mulackstrasse, and he noticed that a motor car was following him. And in this motor car there were two army soldiers from the American base. One of the soldiers rolled down the car window:

(*The* AMERICAN SOLDIER *has a decidedly Midwestern accent.*)

AMERICAN SOLDIER: Hey, can we buy that clock off you?

ALFRED: Not this one; it's mine.

AMERICAN SOLDIER: My mom said I couldn't come home without a clock. One of those Black Forest jobs. Man, that'd look sweet back in Terre Haute.

ALFRED: I do have other clocks I'm willing to sell.

AMERICAN SOLDIER: Oh, yeah?

CHARLOTTE: And the soldiers trooped into Mulackstrasse,

into his apartment, where he had nine or ten regulators for sale.

ALFRED: *(to the two soldiers)* Take your pick.

AMERICAN SOLDIER: Beautiful. We'll take two.

CHARLOTTE: At that time—in the seventies—people thought gaudy old standing clocks were just old-fashioned junk. Kitsch. In Berlin, you could pick up a grandfather clock for, maybe, fifty marks. Very cheap!

AMERICAN SOLDIER: Shit, Sergeant Matheson paid twice that on the Ku'Damm.

(CHARLOTTE does a double take at the SOLDIER, a bit taken aback at his interruption. He cowers apologetically. She continues with her tale.)

CHARLOTTE: Anyway. Not long after that, Alfred came to me with a proposition.

ALFRED: *(the wheeler-dealer)* People are always giving you clocks as gifts. Half the time, you don't want them. They're early twentieth century, and that's too modern for your museum—

CHARLOTTE: Alfred . . . what are you suggesting? . . .

ALFRED: I've got a friend named Edward. He's got an automobile. We can drive to Pankow, to the woods near Weissensee, with the clocks in tow.

CHARLOTTE: *(intrigued in spite of herself)* Yes?

ALFRED: We'll sell a bundle, right out of the back of the car.

CHARLOTTE: Sure enough, the American soldiers came, and they looked into the back of Edward's car.

AMERICAN SOLDIER: These are damn nice.

ALFRED: Why not buy them all, as souvenirs? To send back home. How many have I got here? Nine, ten, eleven . . .

AMERICAN SOLDIER: Hell, our car isn't big enough. *(the glorious dawning of an idea)*

We'll come next week with a little bus.

CHARLOTTE: So we met them again the following week.

AMERICAN SOLDIER: Hey. We're back. *(sotto voce, to his buddy)* See, I told you—*one of these dudes wears a dress.*

CHARLOTTE: Into the bus they put one, two, three, four clocks. And they're prepared to drive across the border, back into Western Berlin.

CUSTOMS OFFICIAL: *Halten Sie, bitte.*

AMERICAN SOLDIER: They can't stop us . . . we're Americans, man.

CUSTOMS OFFICIAL: *Wir müssen diesen Autobus inspizieren.*

AMERICAN SOLDIER: *(to the Customs Official)* Sure, no prob. *(to his fellow soldier)* Hey, Dave. It's friggin' Customs. They want to, like, case our bus . . . You crazy? You tell 'em no. I'm not telling 'em no. Just . . . holy shit . . . *just get out of the goddamn bus.* Come on, man, it's not worth it. They're fuckin' *cuckoo clocks*, for chrissakes.

*(*CHARLOTTE *takes over the narrative again.)*

CHARLOTTE: And they detained the soldiers for six, seven hours. And the border agents wrote down the number of their bus. And the Stasi started keeping a list of all our little sales. And the next time the bus came to meet us they followed it with an automobile of their own. Some months later, Alfred heard a knock on his door.

STASI AGENT: We have reason to believe that you're engaging in illegal sales, with foreign military personnel. We hope—for your sake—we have made a grave error in judgment.

CHARLOTTE: Alfred came back to me. Naturally, I expected him to mend his ways.

ALFRED: *(incorrigible as ever)* Lottchen, I've an idea. Why don't we sell the clocks out of your basement instead of the car?

CHARLOTTE: But Alfred—

ALFRED: There's no other place in all of Eastern Berlin quite so secret.

CHARLOTTE: So Alfred brought the clocks around to my place, and we stashed them here. Right here, in this basement corridor, there were five, six, seven clocks. Standing in the darkness, like sentinels, *ja*?

(The stage is plunged into near-darkness, except for a small light illuminating CHARLOTTE. *We hear the ticking of an enormous clock.)*

And then at midnight:

ALFRED: Lottchen! Open the door! We're in terrible danger.

CHARLOTTE: What now?

ALFRED: They followed us. The Stasi came to my apartment. They tore through my desk, they found Western currency. Tomorrow they're coming to see you!

CHARLOTTE: What can I do, hmm? I'll bolt the door.

ALFRED: Save yourself, Lottchen. Renounce me.

CHARLOTTE: Don't be ridiculous.

ALFRED: Tell them the clocks are mine.

CHARLOTTE: I could never!

ALFRED: Why should we both go to prison?

CHARLOTTE: I won't say such a thing—I *can't*!

ALFRED: They'll force their way into your house. They'll go traipsing into the basement, into the bar. They'll confiscate your Polyphones and your Pianolas—they'll take your sideboard and your *Vertiko* . . .

CHARLOTTE: *Quatsch! Du bist zu dramatisch!*

ALFRED: Listen to me! They'll auction off your entire collection, and all to fill their own fat coffers.

CHARLOTTE: *Das ist nicht möglich. Das können sie nicht tun.*

ALFRED: Your museum will be finished. Through.

(The ear-piercing gong of a clock striking midnight. CHARLOTTE stands, framed by the accusatory white glow of Stasi searchlights.)

CHARLOTTE: So when the Stasi came, that's what I did.

(She sits. A light shines on her from above, like an interrogation. Her voice cracks and her eyes well with tears.)

"These clocks, they do not belong to me. I am only a way station. The collector that you seek . . . the black marketeer . . . his name is Alfred Kirschner."

(The light softens, and CHARLOTTE *resumes the tale.)*

And they arrested him.

(The brutal slam of a prison door. Again, the harsh lines of prison light. ALFRED *pens another note behind bars.)*

ALFRED:
My dear Charlotte,

I've been in jail for one week now. When the Stasi discovered that I was a homosexual, they feared I might be labeled a mental defective, and exempt from a trial. But at the institution Herr Doktor Kreinholz . . . may God damn him forever . . . he said I was perfectly sane. And so I was thrown to the dogs.

You know they perform a strip search when you're being admitted to prison. Needless to say with me, they got a big surprise.

CHARLOTTE: *(reading the letter) Mein Gott!*

(She's amused in spite of herself, and imparts the contents to us with a tiny grin.)

They found a cock ring around Alfred's penis and his nuts. They couldn't get it off, because he had such big private parts. So they sent him to the hospital in the prison to see if they could remove it, but even they couldn't get it off. And finally a metal specialist came, and he slid a piece of metal between Alfred's ring and his sex organs, and then he sawed it off.

ALFRED: What a sad parting, I told the doctor. I've been wearing that sweet little band of steel for over ten years!

CHARLOTTE: I visited Alfred Kirschner in jail. I had on my red coat with the flared skirt, and my hair was quite long.

(She rises to enter the visitation area and is stopped by an OFFICIAL.*)*

PRISON OFFICIAL: Who are you, and who do you intend to visit today?

CHARLOTTE: I am the wife of Alfred Kirschner, of course.

(He admits her, and she sits before ALFRED. *She smiles at him fondly, pressing her hand against the glass that separates them, hoping to impart some small measure of hope.*

ALFRED *slinks back in his chair, dejected.)*

ALFRED: My cell is too damn cold . . . my rheumatism. My knees are brittle, like porcelain.

CHARLOTTE: I've brought you some warm clothes.

ALFRED: Have you heard from Edward? Or Minna Mahlich?

CHARLOTTE: They're all afraid. "Guilt by association." They don't want the Stasi investigating their lives, too.

(CHARLOTTE *returns to us to finish the story.*)

Originally, I intended to burn all of Alfred's letters. I was always afraid if the Stasi searched my house they would find them and ask, "Why do you keep the correspondence of a criminal?" See, the first letter is crinkled. But I rescued it from the wastepaper basket. Because one day I felt I'd be able to tell the truth. And today is that time.

Here . . . written in his own hand, on the back of *eine Speisekarte* . . . a menu from an old restaurant . . .

ALFRED: *(as though it were a love letter)* This is my last will and testament. In the case of my death, I give my entire collection of clocks, records, cylinders, and everything else in my possession to Lothar Berfelde, also known as Charlotte von Mahlsdorf. Affectionately, Alfred Kirschner.

CHARLOTTE: While he was incarcerated, his home was broken into and the Stasi impounded everything that he owned. Just like the Nazis during the deportation of Jewish people, they took all his things.

(She turns in a slow circle, as if gazing upon the ravaged apartment for the first time.)

He was left with only his bed. It was awful. After his release from jail, I went to the church in Weissensee and I found Alfred a place in their nursing home.

(Once again, she tries to appear optimistic.)

One day, Alfred, you'll have your own flat again.

ALFRED: *(bitterly, with contempt)* No. Never again. I don't want to collect anything anymore.

CHARLOTTE: One night the telephone rang. It was *eine Krankenschwester.* A nurse on the line.

NURSE: You must come at once. Alfred died tonight.

CHARLOTTE: It's true, he left me everything. All in this small folder. Here's an old bill from the electric company, one he couldn't pay. Here's a picture of Alfred with an Electrola gramophone. Ah! Yes! An old postage stamp, from East Prussia.

(She picks ALFRED's glasses up off the sideboard and contemplates them a final time.)

Alfred was more intelligent than I.

(She slides open a drawer and—delicately—places the glasses inside, shutting it gently. A burial.)

Still, that's all he had left—scraps of paper, yes?

AKTENVERMERK

(JOHN strides forward, commandeering the scene from CHARLOTTE.)

JOHN: Now, Doug, that's one helluva story. Trouble is, it doesn't scan with the facts in her file. That midnight visit? Alfred's heroic offer to take the fall on her behalf? *He begs her to sing like a bird?* It's like some Cold War thriller written by Armistead Maupin. Even if it did happen, Charlotte was already in deep with the Stasi and had been for at least a year. You think Alfred knew that? Just listen to this:

(A STASI AGENT *appears in a pool of light. He boasts about* CHARLOTTE *to his superior officer.)*

STASI AGENT: We asked the informant—code name "Park"— if he could gather evidence about the suspect Alfred Kirschner. He assured us that he had Herr Kirschner's absolute trust, and could elicit information without arousing his suspicion.

For the past five months, Park has duly recounted conversations with Herr Kirschner directly to us. He has reported Herr Kirschner's illegal transactions with American soldiers. He has confirmed that Herr Kirschner was routinely offered Western currency in exchange for illicit goods. Park has even provided us with five additional names, those of Herr Kirschner's cronies.

Customs officials successfully arrested Alfred Kirschner in the first week of August 1971. We have, of course, granted Park full immunity. He may even merit a promotion.

(The AGENT *disappears.* DOUG *turns to* JOHN *in protest.)*

DOUG: John! We can't go looking to the Stasi file for facts. Those agents had quotas to fill, supervisors to impress. Reports were doctored all the time! One entry contradicts the next.

(The same STASI AGENT reappears. This time he makes profuse apologies to the same superior officer.)

STASI AGENT: Unfortunately, the informant Park is poorly suited for covert operations. He is too easily distracted by old furniture. His manner of dress is willfully bizarre. His penmanship is so slow, so painstaking—so full of curlicues and frippery—that it's futile to ask for written reports. We are reduced to taking dictation. After forty-eight months of service, mountains of paperwork, and numerous visits to the Gründerzeit Museum, he has yielded nothing useful. And so we have decided to terminate our association.

A CONVENIENT LAPSE

DOUG: I went back to Mahlsdorf, file in hand.

(DOUG musters the courage to confront CHARLOTTE.)

Charlotte, I know this is difficult. And I know I'm an American, from thousands of miles away . . . I didn't even really know what the Cold War *was* until it ended . . . so I've no right to sit in judgment. But about Alfred Kirschner . . . his arrest . . .

(CHARLOTTE delicately straightens her pearls.)

CHARLOTTE: Hmm. Yes. Of course.

(Wafting through the air, the sound of ALFRED's old music boxes.)

Here is an old sweater I made for Alfred when he was in prison. And the buttons—the brass buttons—are from the coat of my granduncle, when he served under the Kaiser himself.
DOUG: That's not . . . my question was—
CHARLOTTE: These hands have laid mortar and brick; they have carved walnut. But for Alfred they learned to knit.
DOUG: But, Charlotte, I—
CHARLOTTE: *(beat)* It is beautiful, yes?

(CHARLOTTE seems lost in her own private, hermetically sealed world of denial.

Suddenly, the driving beat of broadcast news music. A square of light—like a television screen—appears, and the GERMAN NEWS ANCHOR steps into it. He double-checks the feed in his ear, then launches into the evening telecast.)

THE CROSS

GERMAN NEWS ANCHOR: Should Charlotte von Mahlsdorf be required to relinquish the Medal of Honor? That question is on the minds of Germans everywhere today as news of Charlotte's Stasi involvement continues to dominate headlines. Conservative politician Markus Kaufmann:

(MARKUS KAUFMANN *leans forward toward an invisible microphone.*)

MARKUS KAUFMANN: It's terrible. It's a tragedy. If anyone suffered because of her cooperation . . . if a human price was paid . . . then of course she should be stripped of the medal. It's a civic honor, not a badge of shame.

GERMAN NEWS ANCHOR: Humboldt University student Ulrike Liptsch:

(ULRIKE *plays with the tips of her long blond hair, then tosses it back over her shoulder. Although she's a serious student of political science, she will one day become a supermodel.*)

ULRIKE LIPTSCH: My friends and I, we think it's stupid. To take away the medal. We shouldn't even look at Charlotte's Stasi files; we should just burn them. One out of every three citizens was working as an informant. Finger-pointing is pointless; it doesn't unify, it only tears people apart.

GERMAN NEWS ANCHOR: Outspoken former political dissident
Josef Rüdiger:

*(JOSEF is a bitter man, with the deep-seated anger that
comes from unspeakable suffering.)*

JOSEF RÜDIGER: I spent two years at the Stasi prison in
Bautzen. They dislocated my shoulders from my sockets;
they forced a catheter up my urinary tract and filled it with
alcohol. And still I uttered no one's name but my own. *(beat)*
Complicity in this country should always be treated as a
criminal act. Hasn't the twentieth century taught us that
much?
GERMAN NEWS ANCHOR: The President's office said the
prestigious medal had been revoked only once before, when a
previous recipient revealed he'd formerly been a member of
the SS.

THE THREE *M*'S

*(CHARLOTTE turns to face her ACCUSERS and says with
severity):*

CHARLOTTE: *(to Marcus Kaufman) Museum. (to Ulrike
Liptsch) Möbel. (to Josef Rüdiger) Männer.*

*(She turns to the audience—all smiles again—to
translate.)*

Museum. Furniture. Men.

(Then back to the unseen chorus of critics in a spirited, vehement defense.)

This is the order in which I have lived my life.

*(*CHARLOTTE *again enlists the audience as her confidant and friend, telling it another of her many tales.)*

One day I had an appointment to visit a clockmaker in Kopenick. And on the way I saw a man. And he said, *"Fräulein, nicht so stolz!"* Lady, not so proud! So I smiled. And I was wearing my leather shorts, and he said to me, "You have such a nice backside. A nice ass for whipping."

And I thought, Yes. And he asked me to go inside the public tramway station, to the toilets. But only a few shops away there was . . . waiting for me . . . *eine alte Standuhr* . . . a standing clock . . . made of oak, with a perfect mechanism from the last century. And to be late for a clockmaker is *unhöflich.* Too impolite.

(Finally, she turns back to her detractors, emphatic once more.)

For me, there was no choice.

(A blast of Euro-pop, and sensationalist, hip talk-show host ZIGGY FLUSS *seizes the stage.)*

CELEBRITY

ZIGGY FLUSS: Good evening, Deutschland, and welcome to the Ziggy Fluss show. I'm Ziggy Fluss. Among tonight's special guests . . . the tiny *Grossmutter* with the great big secret . . . Germany's most controversial transvestite . . . Berlin's own Trannie Granny, Charlotte von Mahlsdorf!

(Applause. CHARLOTTE *enters, caught like a doe in headlights. Hesitantly, she approaches her assigned seat, next to* ZIGGY.*)*

Good evening, Charlotte!
CHARLOTTE: *Guten Abend.*
ZIGGY FLUSS: You're used to the red-hot glare of studio lights, aren't you, Charlotte? You've been on the news, you've done the talk-show circuit.
CHARLOTTE: Yes.
ZIGGY FLUSS: But you still don't own a television, correct?
CHARLOTTE: *Nein.* If I want to look at myself, I look in the mirror, *ja?*
ZIGGY FLUSS: *Wunderschön, wunderschön. Eine gute Antwort!*

(laughter and applause)

Tell me, are the rumors true? Have you really decided to move to Sweden?
CHARLOTTE: I was in Stockholm on a tour for my book—

meine Selbstbiographie—and the people, they have been very kind to me.

ZIGGY FLUSS: What about your furniture, eh? All those Gründerzeit goodies. Any plans to open a new museum in Scandinavia?

CHARLOTTE: Yes, of course. An old friend of mine heard I was leaving town. She said to me, "You can't transplant an old tree." I told her, "I am not a tree. I am a flower. And I always carry my flowerpot with me."

(The studio audience loves it; she's so damned enchanting.)

ZIGGY FLUSS: But Berlin's the city that made you a star! How can you leave her behind?

CHARLOTTE: I'm afraid that there is too much violence here.

ZIGGY FLUSS: And not just on television, am I right?

CHARLOTTE: A short time after I became the *Bundesverdienstkreuz*, we had a garden party in my museum. Almost *achthundert* people, *ja*? We played Donna Summer on the hi-fi, and everyone was dancing and singing under paper lanterns. And I heard a window smash in my basement. A rock. The Brown plague had come back again. *Kristallnacht* once more.

ZIGGY FLUSS: Sure, I read about it. Front page of *Die Morgenpost*. Your museum was vandalized, correct?

CHARLOTTE: The neo-Nazis knew I was a homosexual. They came over the wall—thirty of them—with flare guns and gas pistols. The gays were all cowards, running inside, but the lesbians stayed to fight. And my friend Sylvia, she was in the cellar, trying to shut the door, and she got a gas pistol in the eye. Her retina was damaged. A young girl from Frankfurt an der Oder almost died. They cracked open her cranium with an iron stick.

(ZIGGY FLUSS *swallows. His lightweight show has taken a very sudden, very grave turn.*)

ZIGGY FLUSS: Holy Christ.

(CHARLOTTE—*deep in the story now—rises from her chair, reliving the attack.*)

CHARLOTTE: And I was coming from the cellar with an old pickax, and a skinhead met me on the stair. He had a swastika tattooed on his arm, yes?
FIRST NEO-NAZI: Hitler forgot to shove you in an oven in Sachsenhausen!
CHARLOTTE: And I swung and hit the blade in the old banister, splitting it open like a sapling, *ja*? And from behind me, another *laut* voice.
SECOND NEO-NAZI: We should drown you in the Ostsee!
CHARLOTTE: And there was a second, *mit einem Schlagholz*; a club. And I said, "I have met you before! When I was sixteen years old!"
     And then *die Polizei* came. And the young men scattered. Like *die Asche*, after a fire. No one was arrested. No one went to jail.

(A pause. CHARLOTTE *takes her seat again.*

Even the pathologically upbeat ZIGGY *is momentarily wiped out by the raw power of her story.)*

ZIGGY FLUSS: *(under his breath)* Wow. *Autsch! Die Brutalität. Solche Brutalität.*

CHARLOTTE: My old Victrola, it was smashed. Broken bottles. Electric wires on the ground.

ZIGGY FLUSS: Young people today. It's bad, isn't it? They're hurting, they're disillusioned. They've been promised so much, especially in the East. Reunification. Now they feel they've been had.

CHARLOTTE: It's no excuse.

ZIGGY FLUSS: *(chastened)* No, you can't make excuses, can you?

CHARLOTTE: *Nein. Niemals.*

In Solingen, Turkish women getting burned out of their homes. Asylum seekers from Yugoslavia being beaten on the streets. Anti-Semitism has come back. So has homophobia. Every day, new threats.

ZIGGY FLUSS: Keep talking, Charlotte, and I'll move, too! Ibiza, or maybe Mykonos, right?

(A quick spasm of laughter from the studio; ZIGGY *silences it with a look. He has a hard-hitting question to ask now.)*

Now, Charlotte . . . you know Ziggy has to ask. Your flight from Berlin happens to coincide with recent, widely

published news reports about your Stasi involvement. Some of your critics suggest that you'd rather skip town than face the prospect of a tarnished reputation here at home.
CHARLOTTE: Hmm. Yes. Of course.

(CHARLOTTE smiles sweetly and answers in careful, deliberate tones.)

   In Mahlsdorf, my museum had twenty-three rooms. In Porla-Brunn, I will have only eight. But that is good for a woman my age, yes? Not so much furniture to dust.

(She looks searchingly at the audience for the same warm smiles—the same compassion—her wonderful anecdotes always engender. It's hard to tell . . . has she won her listeners over yet again? Or is she being met by stony silence?

Quietly, compassionately—almost apologetically—ZIGGY places a hand on her knee.)

ZIGGY FLUSS: *Fantastisch,* Charlotte, *wirklich Fantastisch.* You'll come back and visit us again, won't you?
CHARLOTTE: *Danke schön.*
ZIGGY FLUSS: We'll be back after a short break, with American singing sensation David Hasselhoff.

EDITORIALS: A PHANTASMAGORIA

(As CHARLOTTE *makes a beeline for her waiting limousine, she's beset by reporters.)*

BRIGITTE KLENSCH: *(chasing after Charlotte)* Excuse me, Frau von Mahlsdorf. Brigitte Klensch, journalist, Berlin. You say you murdered your father. Has anyone inquired after his death certificate? Court records from your trial?

CHARLOTTE: Pardon me, please. *Mein Auto*—the driver, he is waiting.

BRIGITTE KLENSCH: To date, I've found nothing to confirm your claims.

CHARLOTTE: *(evasively)* In the war, such records, they were lost, yes? Flying through the air like burning leaves . . .

KARL HENNING: Charlotte! Karl Henning, from Munich. Isn't it true that the Stasi hired you to appraise furniture?

CHARLOTTE: I remember 1945 like it was only yesterday, but if you ask me, "What did you have for breakfast?" I don't know!

KARL HENNING: According to records we've obtained, you valued furnishings torn from the homes of dissidents, of political prisoners, of the wronged and the oppressed.

CHARLOTTE: You are from the West, yes? Did the Stasi ever come to your door? Tell me, I ask you!

FRANÇOIS GARNIER: François Garnier, Paris. Did the Stasi really pay you in contraband?

CHARLOTTE: I took nothing!

FRANÇOIS GARNIER: Not even an inkwell, a cigarette box for your museum?

CHARLOTTE: *(vehemently)* As a mother would take an orphan child, yes?

SHIRLEY BLACKER: *(very Brooklyn)* Shirley Blacker, New York City. Why do you suppose the public accepted your story with so little scrutiny?

CHARLOTTE: Please! I am old—so old—*I am tired* . . .

DAISUKE YAMAGISHI: Daisuke Yamagishi, Tokyo. Is it true your family considers you a public embarrassment? That even your own brother refutes your claims?

MARK FINLEY: *(gay activist)* Mark Finley, San Francisco. We—as homosexuals— have been systematically denied our own history. Our own past. Perhaps that's why we're so eager to embrace a martyr, even when she's made of glass?

PRADEEP GUPTA: Pradeep Gupta, Bombay. Is it true that you're really a woman after all?

CLIVE TWIMBLEY: *(a heated East Ender)* Clive Twimbley, London. Did you know that the very man responsible for your medal recently told this newspaper—and I quote— "Whenever Charlotte von Mahlsdorf opens her mouth to yawn, she's already begun to lie."

(CHARLOTTE pauses, stunned, more accustomed to adoration than to such vicious censure. She turns to the throng, and says with quiet intensity, as a balm to soothe herself):

CHARLOTTE: When I was almost forty years old, my mother was doing the laundry, yes? Hanging my stockings and my garters on the line. And she turned to me, and she said,

"Lottchen, it's all very well to play dress-up. But now you've grown into a man. When will you marry?"

(She raises her eyes to look at them, each in turn.)

And I said to her, "Never, my dear Mutti. *Ich bin meine eigene Frau.* I am my own wife."

(A PSYCHIATRIST *steps forward to "settle" the matter with science.)*

DIAGNOSIS

DIETER JORGENSEN: Dieter Jorgensen, psychiatrist, Bonn. Berlin's most notorious transvestite is neither a raconteur nor Machiavellian; she is, in fact, mentally ill. Charlotte von Mahlsdorf suffers from autism. Listen to the manner in which she recounts her stories: in a highly ritualized, cadenced way, less to communicate content than to provide a kind of rhythmic reassurance to the chaos in her psyche. This is true of autistic adults; repetition is a palliative. Her stories aren't lies per se; they're self-medication.

ABDICATION

(We join DOUG *in the middle of an impassioned, climactic argument with* JOHN MARKS.*)*

DOUG: So, at the end of the day, what have I got? A shoebox full of scratchy audiotapes. A used copy of *Die Transvestiten*. Enormous personal bias. Not to mention, my German *sucks*.

JOHN: I say, you go with what's in plain, old-fashioned black and white. The press reports, the file—

DOUG: But I need to believe in her stories as much as she does! I need to believe that—a long time ago, in an attic—a generous aunt handed her confused nephew a book and a blessing. That a little boy—*in his mother's housecoat*—survived *storm troopers*. That Lothar Berfelde navigated a path between the two most repressive regimes the Western world has ever known—the *Nazis* and the *Communists*—in a pair of heels. I need to believe that things like that are true. That they can happen in the world.

JOHN: So, what're you gonna do?

DOUG: I don't have a clue. I'm curating her now, and I don't have the faintest idea what to edit and what to preserve.

(Suddenly, from the recesses of the past, an idea. A memory of something said.)

Tape Eight. March 4, 1993.

(DOUG turns to CHARLOTTE to proffer a query.)

Charlotte, what do you do when a piece loses its luster? Are you ever tempted to strip the wood or replace the veneer?

ON CURATING

CHARLOTTE: I did not refinish the pieces. No. *Diese alte
Anrichte?* The polish is as old as the object itself. It is
antique, too.

*(*CHARLOTTE *approaches the miniature museum; she
takes out the large, velvet-lined box. She picks up the tiny
Vertiko.)*

Nicks and cuts. Stains. Cracks.

*(She places it tenderly in the box. Next, a tiny
sideboard.)*

A missing balustrade, a broken spindle. These things, they
are proof of its history. And so you must leave it.

*(She places it snugly in the box, too. Then the small sofa;
the doll-size chair.)*

The furniture in my museum is more than one century
old. People sat on it, slept on it, wrote letters on it, ate
from it.

(She tucks away the kitchen contraption.)

People tried to burn it. In Nazi times. In Stasi times.

(The bust of Kaiser Wilhelm II. The regulator.)

And still, it is standing. It was not only decoration. It was used.

*(*DOUG *passes a diminutive phonograph to her.)*

DOUG: Does a piece ever get so old—so damaged—that you throw it away?

(She takes it from him and places it in the box, too.)

CHARLOTTE: *Nein.* You must save everything. And you must show it—*auf Englisch,* we say—"as is."

(She closes the lid with finality.)

It is a record, yes? Of living. Of lives.

*(*CHARLOTTE *removes her kerchief and becomes* DOUG. *As he speaks,* DOUG *unclasps* CHARLOTTE'*s pearls from around his neck.*

He places them gently on top of the furniture box.)

DOUG: Charlotte von Mahlsdorf did, in fact, move to Sweden, where she lived for almost seven years. But in April of 2002 she decided to take a holiday, to fly back to Berlin—a homecoming of sorts. While visiting her beloved Gründerzeit

Museum, she suffered a heart attack. Alone in a garden of gramophone horns, she died. A few days after her funeral, an envelope arrived in my mailbox; I recognized her familiar script. But no letter. Instead, she'd enclosed a single photograph, sepia with age. In it she's a child. A boy. Lothar Berfelde, at ten years old.

BETWEEN TWO TIGERS

(DOUG *crosses to the center of the room, entering a pool of light.)*

He's at the zoo in Berlin. He's wearing a sailor suit, with a blue collar and matching cuffs. His ears are sticking out at an angle; he's got a very adorable smile. He's on a bench.

Sitting on either side of him, two tigers. Cubs, sure, but they're still as big as he is. And they're not fond of posing, either. Their eyes are dangerously alert. At any moment, they might revolt; they might scratch or bite.

(He says with awe):

But Lothar has one arm around each tiger, and they're resting their forepaws on his knees.

(DOUG *walks over to the phonograph and places the needle on the wax cylinder.*

*Through its horn, the sound of an original, taped
interview with* CHARLOTTE VON MAHLSDORF, *made in 1993
on a scratchy microcassette.*

The sound quality is poor, but the words are intelligible.)

TAPE RECORDING: *(the voice of* DOUG*)* Tape Four with
Charlotte von Mahlsdorf, February 2nd, 1993. I'm on the way
to Mahlsdorf to meet with her now.

*(A soft click as the tape recorder is turned off, then on
again.)*

TAPE RECORDING: *(the voice of* CHARLOTTE*)* Now this is the
first room of the museum. And this here is a little
phonograph, and on this record you see a picture of Thomas
Alva Edison. And he was the inventor of the first talking
machine of the world, in July of 1877. And the record is made
by the National Phonograph Company in Orange, New Jersey.

(On the recording, we hear CHARLOTTE *place the needle
on the Edison wax roll. The needle idles a moment, then
we hear the tinny, glorious sound of an old-fashioned
waltz.*

DOUG *stands, listening.*

Fade out.)